YA
618.92
GRA

18090
12.90

Gravelle, Karen
  Understanding birth
  defects

DATE DUE			
OCT 2 8 1992			

Buena Vista Public Library
Buena Vista, Colo.

UNDERSTANDING
BIRTH DEFECTS

UNDERSTANDING
BIRTH DEFECTS
KAREN GRAVELLE

FRANKLIN WATTS   1990
NEW YORK   LONDON   TORONTO   SYDNEY

To Dr. Radoslav Jovanovic

Photographs courtesy of:
Photo Researchers: pp.16, 19 (all Leonard Lessin),
27 (Dick Hanley), 43 (Sherry Suris), 51 (Bob Combs), 57
(Lynn McLaren), 63, 79 (both Nancy Durrell), 65 (Stephen L.
Feldman), 87 (Blair Seitz), 101 (Alexander Tsiaras), 113 (Bruce Roberts);
Reuters/Bettmann Newsphotos: p. 47; UPI/Bettmann Newsphotos: p. 84;
March of Dimes Birth Defect Foundation: p. 90.

Library of Congress Cataloging-in-Publication Data

Gravelle, Karen.
Understanding birth defects / Karen Gravelle.
p.   cm.
Contents: Includes bibliographical references.
Summary: Examines the causes of birth defects, the hardships faced
by children born with them, and ways of preventing them.
ISBN 0-531-10955-0
1. Abnormalities, Human—Etiology—Juvenile literature.
2. Prenatal care—Juvenile literature.   3. Handicapped children—
Care—Juvenile literature. [1. Abnormalities, Human.   2. Birth
injuries.   3. Physically handicapped.   4. Mentally handicapped.]
I. Title.
RG626.G73   1990
618.92′0043—dc20   90-32658   CIP   AC

Copyright © 1990 by Karen Gravelle
All rights reserved
Printed in the United States
6 5 4 3 2 1

CONTENTS

UNDERSTANDING
BIRTH DEFECTS

INTRODUCTION:
WHAT ARE BIRTH DEFECTS?

Most people have had experience with birth defects. For some, this experience may have come through knowing someone, a friend or classmate, with a congenital visual impairment or sickle-cell anemia. Others may have members of their own families with a birth defect, perhaps one of the more common disorders like clubfoot or Down's syndrome. At a minimum, the majority of people have probably passed individuals on the street who have easily recognized birth disorders such as dwarfism or hydrocephalus.

Even people who think they have never encountered someone with a birth defect are likely to be wrong. Since 250,000 babies with birth defects of varying severity are born in the United States *each year,* [1] it would be hard to not meet some of these people. But because many defects are not visible, it is not always possible for others to know whether someone is affected or not. In some cases, such as cleft lip or congenital heart defects, the problem may have been surgically repaired during infancy, leaving only tiny scars that are barely detectable. In other instances—Duchenne muscular dystrophy, for example—an affected child may seem perfectly normal at birth, but as the damage caused by the defect accumulates, the effects of the disorder slowly become evident. In some disorders, this may take six months, four years, or, in the case of a few defects, three or four decades.

In spite of the many types of birth defects and the varying degrees of disability they cause, all birth defects have certain features in common. By definition, they are all either structural abnormalities or biochemical disorders that are present, although not necessarily obvious, at birth. They can be caused by many things: heredity, prenatal exposure to dangerous aspects of the environment, accidents during delivery, or some combination of the above. Understanding these defects—what causes them, how to prevent them, and what to do for people who have them—is what this book is all about.

In addition to birth defects, this book is about one other serious problem as well. Referred to as low birth weight, this condition is not technically a birth defect. But since low birth weight is related to 70 percent of all infant deaths,[2] it can be just as devastating as any birth disorder. For a number of reasons, teenage mothers are more likely than other women to give birth to babies with low birth weight. Because this condition is often a result of a mother's activities during pregnancy, the problem can frequently be prevented. Thus, it's especially important for young women to learn about low birth weight and its causes.

10

PART ONE:
WHAT CAUSES
BIRTH DEFECTS?

Birth defects can occur for many reasons. In hereditary disorders, a child inherits abnormal genetic material from one or both parents. Thus, the defect is present from conception, although evidence of the disorder may not be apparent until an affected person reaches childhood or, occasionally, even adulthood.

In other instances, a genetically normal baby may be permanently damaged before birth by exposure to dangerous substances in the environment. These environmental attacks may be in the form of radiation, alcohol, infectious disease, or drugs, or they may come from sources that we are unaware are harmful.

Not surprisingly, birth defects often arise from a combination of hereditary and environmental factors. In some instances, environmental factors may damage the genes in a parent's reproductive cells. Although this may not affect the parent's own health, the defective genes can be passed on to the next generation. In other situations, an infant's genetic makeup may leave the baby more vulnerable to certain aspects of the environment.

The better we understand the causes of birth defects and low birth weight, the more effective we can be in predicting, preventing, and treating these conditions.

11

1

HEREDITARY BIRTH DEFECTS

Hereditary, or genetically caused, birth defects result from abnormal genes inherited from one or both parents. Sometimes the disorder is caused by a single defective gene—only one of the seventy-five thousand to one hundred thousand genes each of us carries.[1] Other birth defects occur as a result of problems with entire chromosomes, the forty-six threads of material on which genes are located. Most birth defects occur in all races and both sexes. Some, however, are more prevalent among certain ethnic groups. A few defects strike only males, and in at least one condition, only females are affected.

CHROMOSOMAL DEFECTS

Bob and Janette were elated. After almost five years of trying to conceive, Janette had finally become pregnant. Mixed with their feelings of excitement, however, was a small, nagging fear. Janette was thirty-seven years old, and she and Bob knew this placed her at greater risk of having a child with a birth defect known as Down's syndrome. One of the most common birth defects, Down's syndrome affects people of all ethnic groups. Children with this disorder suffer from varying degrees of mental retardation and a range of physical deformities. Bob and Janette were not sure they could handle a child with serious abnormalities. Adding to their anxiety was the knowledge that they probably would not have another chance to have their own baby.

As far as they knew, no one in either Janette's or Bob's family had ever had Down's syndrome. How, then, could they have a child with it? What does Janette's age have to do with whether or not her baby is born with these defects? Bob is even older than his wife. Shouldn't the father's age matter too? Would the situation be different if Janette had already had children?

Since the only way a trait can be inherited is through our genes, it's important to understand what genes are and how they work in order to answer these questions. Genes are the blueprints from which we are constructed. Each pair of genes carries instructions for the manufacture of a particular protein needed to build or to run our bodies. Because each pair of genes has the directions for only one type of protein, it takes thousands and thousands of genes to make our bodies. Although some of our traits are determined by one pair of genes, most require the input of many genes.

Genes are located on chromosomes, which are long threadlike structures contained in the nucleus of each cell. Each species has a specific number of chromosomes. Humans have forty-six chromosomes, or twenty-three pairs, in each cell of the body, except the sperm and egg cells. One of each of these pairs comes from a person's mother; the other one in the pair comes from his or her father.

In twenty-two of these pairs, each chromosome resembles its twin; these chromosomes are called autosomes. However, the two chromosomes that compose the twenty-third pair in every cell look very

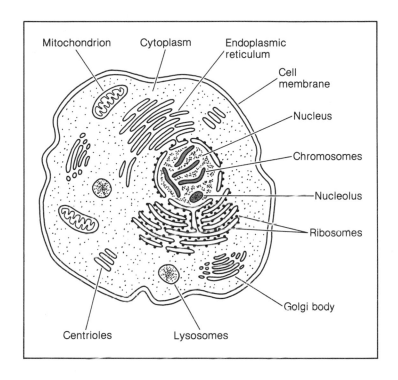

A diagram of a cell

different from each other. Called the X and the Y chromosomes because one looks like an X and the other looks like a Y, they determine a person's sex and are called sex chromosomes. The X chromosome is about twice as large as the Y chromosome and has an additional arm. Females have two X chromosomes; males have an X and a Y chromosome.

   With the exception of eggs and sperm, each cell in the body has forty-six chromosomes. Because egg and sperm cells are designed to fuse with each other, they each have only twenty-three chromosomes, half of each pair of chromosomes. When they fuse at fertilization, they form one cell that again has the characteristic species number, forty-six. Problems can

15

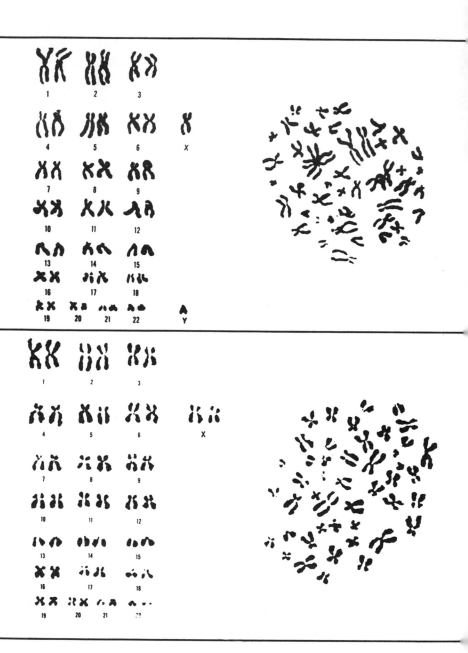

These karotypes show normal male
and normal female chromosomes.

occur, however, when the chromosomes are dividing in half to form an egg or a sperm, and these problems can result in birth defects. One of the things that can go wrong is that the cell may divide unequally, a process called nondisjunction. This is what happens in most cases (90 percent) of Down's syndrome.

In Down's syndrome, as one cell is dividing to form two sex cells, the #21 chromosome pair does not divide normally, and both chromosomes end up in one cell. Thus, instead of both sex cells having twenty-three chromosomes, one has twenty-four and the other has twenty-two. Because the loss of an entire chromosome is usually lethal, the cell with only twenty-two chromosomes dies. But the cell having the extra chromosome can survive.

Although this unequal division can happen when either a sperm or an egg is formed, it occurs far more frequently in the formation of an egg. Approximately 70 percent of the individuals with Down's syndrome acquired it as a result of nondisjunction in the formation of the egg, compared to 20 percent who acquired it as a result of nondisjunction in the formation of the sperm.[2] (The remaining 10 percent are cases that result from other problems in cell division.) Because nondisjunction is more likely to happen in eggs than in sperm, Janette's age is more important than Bob's in determining the couple's chance of having an affected child.

As a woman gets older, the risk of nondisjunction increases. Between the ages of twenty and twenty-five, her chance of having a child with Down's syndrome is only one in two thousand. By the time she reaches thirty-five, however, the risk will be one in four hundred, and at age forty-five it will have leaped to one in thirty-two.[3] The mother's age, not how many children she's had, is the factor that makes nondisjunction more likely. Janette would face the same risk regardless of whether or not this was her first child.

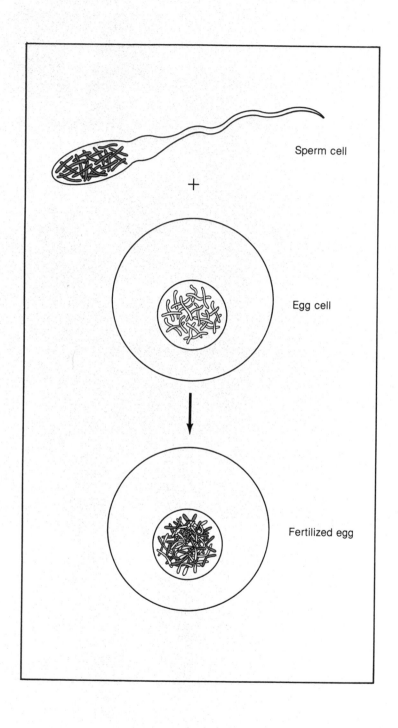

Sperm cell

+

Egg cell

Fertilized egg

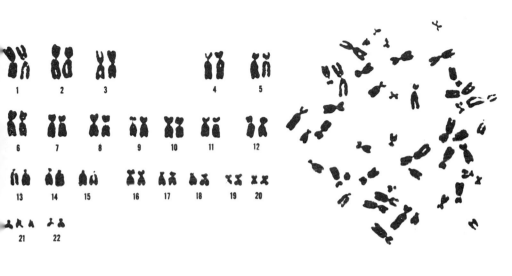

Note the three number 21 chromosomes
of this boy with Down's syndrome.

What happens when an egg with an additional #21 chromosome is fertilized? Instead of forty-six chromosomes, the resulting cell will have a total of forty-seven. Because thousands of genes are involved, the impact of having an extra chromosome is extensive.

Down's syndrome is a good example of the many things that can go wrong as a result of having a chromosomal abnormality. Children with this disorder have short stature; oblique, slanting eyelids; a broad, flat nose; a large tongue; small, low-set ears; and short stubby fingers. All suffer from some degree of mental retardation, which can vary from moderate to severe.

Some individuals with this syndrome have other problems as well. Congenital heart defects are common. Children with Down's syndrome typically have narrow ear canals and a strong tendency for middle ear infections. As a result, more than 75 percent of the infants born with Down's syndrome have some form of hearing loss. Finally, approximately 10 percent of the infants born with Down's syndrome have a narrowing of the intestines. If this defect is not surgically corrected, the child will starve to death within the first weeks of life.

In addition to nondisjunction, other events can damage a chromosome. In the process of forming new cells, a piece of one chromosome may stick to a completely different chromosome, ripping off and remaining attached to the second chromosome. In other cases, a segment of a chromosome or even a whole chromosome is lost. Because so many genes are affected when a chromosomal abnormality occurs, the result is usually death. Over 50 percent of the infants that are miscarried before twelve weeks have chromosomal defects.[4]

Although the loss of an entire chromosome is usually fatal, there is one exception—Turner's syndrome. Turner's syndrome affects only females. Patty is one of these individuals. She is missing one of the two chromosomes that determine a person's sex; specifically, she is missing one X chromosome.

At eight years old, Patty is very short for her age and has a webbed neck. Other than that, she doesn't look much different from other children. She doesn't act differently either. Although not at the top of her third-grade class, Patty is of normal intelligence and is doing well in school.

When she reaches adolescence, however, the effects of Patty's missing chromosome will become more noticeable. Her breasts will remain underdeveloped, and because she lacks functional ovaries, she will not begin to menstruate. Like other women with Turner's syndrome, she will never be able to have children.

Although these are serious problems, they are certainly not as severe as those faced by people with Down's syndrome. How come Patty doesn't have more damaging effects? In fact, how come Patty is alive at all?

The reason a child like Patty can survive with one X chromosome, whereas the loss of a chromosome from any of the other twenty-two pairs would be fatal, is that females have two X chromosomes, while males have one X and one Y chromosome. Thus, females have an extra X chromosome to start with. As far as we know, the Y chromosome is responsible only for directing the development of male sexual organs. Although genes that affect some nonsexual traits are located on the X chromosome, males (with one X and one Y chromosome) are proof that one X chromosome is enough for the normal development of these nonsexual traits. Unfortunately, however, one X chromosome is not enough to direct the full development of female sexual organs. Thus, girls born with only one X chromosome do not mature sexually and can never have children.

Other chromosomal abnormalities involving the X and Y chromosomes can also occur. The total absence of X chromosomes is lethal, so no individuals having just a Y chromosome survive. But there are people who have extra sex chromosomes. Individuals with two X chromosomes and one Y chromosome have a condition called Kleinfelter's syndrome. Since these individuals have a Y chromosome, they are male. Like females with Turner's syndrome, these men usually have normal intelligence, but are sterile. They typically have small testes, enlarged breasts, and sparse body hair. An extra Y chromosome has different effects. Men who have two Y chromosomes and one X chromosome are usually taller than average, and their sexual development is normal. They are generally of lower intelligence, however.

AUTOSOMAL DOMINANT DISORDERS

Jason isn't concerned with the possibility of having a child with a birth defect. At ten years old, he isn't interested in girls yet, much less in having children. Instead, Jason worries that he and his father are going to die. His father has begun to show signs of the fatal hereditary disorder, Huntington's disease, that killed Jason's grandmother. Jason knows that if his father has the disease, there's a 50 percent chance that he has inherited it as well.

Blood tests might be able to determine whether or not Jason's father has Huntington's disease, but so far he has refused to be tested. Unfortunately, there is no treatment for this condition. If he is doomed to have what will be a very unpleasant illness and death, Jason's father doesn't really want to know just yet. Remembering how his grandmother suffered, Jason doesn't really blame him.

If a birth defect is a disorder that is present at birth, how could Jason's father have a birth defect and, at forty years of age, still not know it? Why does Jason have a fifty percent chance of inheriting the disorder if his father does have the disease?

The answer to the first of these questions is relatively simple. In many birth defects, the abnormality is present at birth, but the damage caused by the defect is not noticeable until later in the person's life. The symptoms of sickle cell anemia and Tay-Sachs disease, for example, usually don't appear before an infant is six months old. With other defects, it may take

22

even longer for the disorder to become obvious. Some cases of cystic fibrosis are not diagnosed until the child is four, and symptoms of Duchenne-type muscular dystrophy usually don't show up until ages six to nine.

Huntington's disease is very unusual in the length of time it takes for symptoms to appear. Throughout childhood and early adulthood, there are no visible indications of the disease, and affected individuals lead healthy, normal lives. Somewhere between ages thirty-five and forty-five, however, subtle signs that something is wrong begin to appear in the form of clumsiness or tics (tiny abnormal movements). These neurological disturbances gradually progress, leading to more exaggerated movements. As time goes by, the victim's face becomes twisted with tics and the body writhes uncontrollably.

Coupled with the physical symptoms of Huntington's disease are serious psychological and emotional disturbances that may resemble manic depression or schizophrenia. People afflicted with this condition deteriorate for ten to twenty years, until they finally die. No wonder the prospect that he or his father might have this disorder terrifies Jason!

Jason's likelihood of inheriting Huntington's disease has to do with the ways in which genes interact with one another in determining a trait. Except for a few genes on the X chromosome, each of us inherits two genes for every trait, one gene from our mother and one from our father. These genes can interact in several ways. In one type of interaction, each of the two genes has equal influence. This kind of interaction is responsible for many of our traits, but it's easier to observe in flowers. For example, if crossing a red flower with a white flower results in a pink offspring, then the red and white genes have equal influence in determining color.

In many cases, however, the influence of one gene dominates that of the other. All of the genetic defects discussed in this section, as well as many normal traits, result from this kind of interaction. A familiar example of this interaction is eye color in humans. A brown-eyed person and a blue-eyed person may have either brown-eyed or blue-eyed children but not something in between (although many different shades of brown and blue are possible).

In Huntington's disease, the abnormal, or disease-causing, gene is dominant over the normal gene. Since the effects of the abnormal gene are stronger than those of the normal gene, anyone who inherits one abnormal gene will develop the disorder. Conditions that result from a dominant abnormal gene are called autosomal dominant disorders.

Assuming Jason's father does have Huntington's disease, why does Jason have a 50 percent chance of having inherited it himself? There is no chance Jason's mother has the disease, so Jason could have inherited only a normal gene from her. On the other hand, if Jason's father has Huntington's disease, he might have passed on to Jason either a normal recessive gene or a dominant, disease-causing gene. Because these two genes each had an equal chance of being passed on to Jason, Jason has a 50 percent chance of having inherited the gene for Huntington's disease and, since the gene is dominant, thus has a 50 percent chance of having the disorder.

Unlike Huntington's disease, most autosomal dominant disorders are not fatal. This is because anyone having a fatal dominant gene usually dies long before becoming old enough to have children. With no one to pass it on, the disease-causing fatal gene soon disappears from the population. Huntington's disease is an exception because affected individuals don't begin to have symptoms until they're in their thirties or forties,

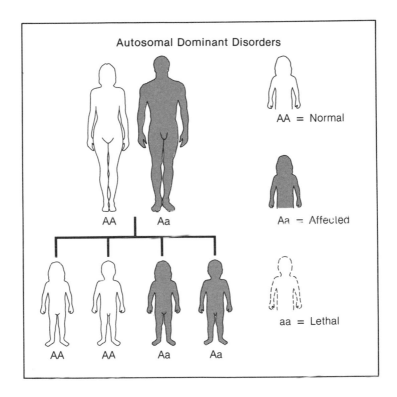

Autosomal Dominant Disorders

AA = Normal

Aa = Affected

aa = Lethal

AA | Aa

AA   AA   Aa   Aa

well after many have already passed the gene on to their children.

Huntington's disease is unusual in another respect as well. Ordinarily, autosomal dominant disorders involve obvious abnormalities in a person's physical structure. Neurofibromatosis, the "Elephant Man's" disease, and achondroplasia, a form of dwarfism, are two examples.

As one of the most common genetic disorders, neurofibromatosis occurs in every racial and ethnic group throughout the world. Its effects can range from severely disabling to mildly disfiguring to so minimal that the condition goes undetected. Fortunately, the kind of deformity portrayed in the movie *The Elephant*

Man is very rare. In fact, most affected individuals have only mild symptoms and live normal lives.

Neurofibromatosis gets its name from the one to a thousand small tumors made up of nerve cells that develop in people afflicted with this condition. Appearing as lumps under the skin, the tumors may be few and barely noticeable or extensive and quite disfiguring. Tumors can also occur on auditory or optic nerves, where they may cause deafness or blindness. Some children with the disorder develop curvature of the spine or learning disabilities, depending on where the tumors develop. While these tumors can appear at any age, they tend to increase during adolescence and pregnancy. As might be expected, individuals with noticeably disfiguring tumors often have psychological problems as well.

Like neurofibromatosis, achondroplasia also occurs in all races. Portrayed by ancient Egyptian artists, this form of dwarfism is one of the oldest recorded birth defects. Children with achondroplasia have a torso of relatively normal proportions, but their arms and legs, particularly the upper arms and the thighs, are abnormally short. Usually, they also have large heads and prominent foreheads and are sway-backed and bowlegged.

Even though neurofibromatosis and achondroplasia result from an abnormal dominant gene inherited from a parent, that parent may not have the disease. Since anyone who inherits a dominant abnormal gene is supposed to have the disorder, this may seem impossible. In some cases, however, the parent who has the gene didn't inherit it but *acquired* it after birth.

Genetic changes, or mutations, can occur in any cell in the body and at any time during a person's life. These mutations can happen spontaneously, or they may result from exposure to radiation, viruses, or other elements in the environment. Because the altered, or

26

This man and his twin brother (who also has achondroplasia) own and operate a gas station in Massachusetts.

abnormal, gene was not part of the original genetic makeup that guided the development of the parent's own body, he or she was unaffected. But mutations that occur in sperm or egg cells can be passed on to the next generation. Over 80 percent of the cases of achondroplasia and about 50 percent of the cases of neurofibromatosis are the result of new mutations in a parent's reproductive cells.[5]

AUTOSOMAL RECESSIVE DISORDERS

In Huntington's disease, neurofibromatosis, and achondroplasia, the defective gene is dominant. But abnormal genes can be recessive too. When a birth defect is caused by an abnormal recessive gene, the condition is called an autosomal recessive disorder.

Conditions inherited through recessive genes differ from autosomal dominant disorders in a number of ways. The most important of these is that because the defective gene is recessive, a person must inherit two abnormal genes—one from each parent—in order to have the disorder. Since the effects of the normal gene override those of the abnormal gene, individuals having one normal and one abnormal gene do not inherit the disorder. But because the abnormal gene is part of their genetic makeup, they can pass it on to their children. Individuals who do not have the disorder themselves but who have an abnormal gene are referred to as carriers.

Sandra is afraid that she may be one of these carriers, and the possibility has raised conflicts for her about her upcoming marriage. Although she loves her fiancé, Arnie, very much, she knows that he wants to have children. Sandra is not sure that she does. She'd like to be a mother, but she's very fearful of having a child like her younger brother, who was born with Tay-Sachs disease.

Sandra vividly remembers how happy she was to have a baby brother and what a beautiful, healthy little boy he was at first. Then, at about six months of age, her brother began to change. He stopped smiling, crawling, and turning over, and he lost his ability to grasp objects or to reach out. Over the next few years, he gradually became paralyzed and blind. Finally, he became so afflicted that he was completely unaware of anything or anyone around him. Then, just before his fourth birthday, he died.

What could possibly cause such devastating changes in an apparently normal child? In the case of Tay-Sachs disease, children who inherit two recessive genes are unable to produce an enzyme that normally breaks down fatty deposits in the brain and nerve cells. With time, these cells become so clogged with fat that they are unable to function. Sadly, there is no treatment available that can cure Tay-Sachs disease or stop it from progressing further.

Because the few facilities that existed to care for children with Tay-Sachs were extremely expensive, Sandra's brother remained at home. Sandra clearly recalls how painful it was to watch him deteriorate and how helpless she felt, knowing nothing could be done for him. But even after her brother had passed away, the disease continued to tear away at her family. The fear that they might have another affected child strained her parents' marriage. For most of her life, it seemed to Sandra that her mother and father were two strangers who just happened to be sharing the same house. Sandra would rather not marry Arnie than to have something like that happen to their relationship.

Does Sandra have reason to worry that she and Arnie might have a child with this disease? If so, what are the chances this could happen? Tay-Sachs disease is an autosomal recessive disorder most prevalent among Jewish people of Central or Eastern European descent. Approximately one of every

29

twenty-five American Jews carries the Tay-Sachs gene.[6] Even if Sandra does have this gene, both she and Arnie would have to be carriers in order for their child to inherit the disease. Since Arnie's ancestors, like Sandra's, were Polish Jews, there is a chance that he could be a carrier as well.

Three possibilities exist in terms of Sandra's and Arnie's genetic makeup, each of which is associated with a different risk of having an affected child. One is that neither Sandra nor Arnie has the recessive gene for Tay-Sachs disease. In that case, none of their children can inherit the condition.

A second possibility is that one of them is a carrier and the other is not. If this is the case, each of the couple's children will inherit at least one normal dominant gene from the parent who has only normal genes. Thus, none of their children will actually have the disease. With each pregnancy, however, there is a 50 percent chance that the child will inherit an abnormal gene from the parent who is a carrier. This means that there is a 50 percent chance that the child will have two normal genes and a 50 percent chance that it will be a carrier.

In both of the cases above, no child will actually inherit the defect. The problem comes when both parents are carriers. In this case, a child has a 25 percent chance of inheriting two normal genes, a 50 percent chance of inheriting one normal and one abnormal gene and being a carrier, and a 25 percent chance of inheriting two abnormal genes and having the disease.

In all autosomal recessive disorders, there is one chance in four that two carriers will have an affected child. This risk is the same for each pregnancy, regardless of whether or not the parents have already had an affected child. Chance has no memory. Two carriers who have already had an affected child should not assume that their next three children will be nor-

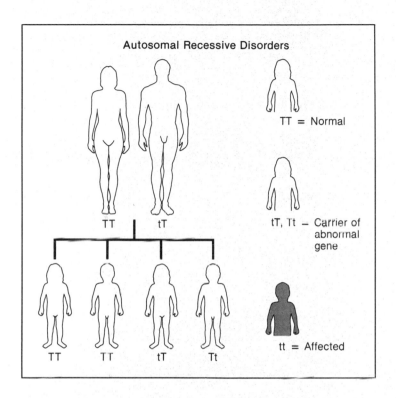

Autosomal Recessive Disorders

TT = Normal

tT, Tt — Carrier of abnormal gene

tt = Affected

mal. On the other hand, if they have had three normal children, this does not necessarily mean that their fourth child will be affected.

Cystic fibrosis and sickle-cell anemia are also autosomal recessive disorders and are inherited in the same manner as Tay-Sachs disease. Cystic fibrosis is the most common fatal genetic disease among Caucasians, and approximately one of every twenty to twenty-five white people carries the cystic fibrosis gene.[7] Infants with cystic fibrosis are very susceptible to lung disease and have bacterial lung infections throughout their lives. In addition, affected children secrete a thick mucus that clogs the airways of their lungs. These two conditions result in the breakdown of

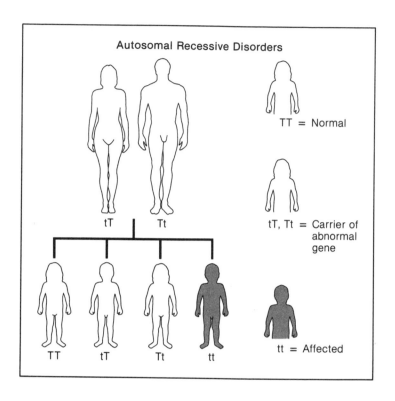

Autosomal Recessive Disorders

TT = Normal

tT, Tt = Carrier of abnormal gene

tt = Affected

tT   Tt

TT   tT   Tt   tt

the airway walls. As a result, most people with cystic fibrosis eventually die of respiratory failure. Excess secretions can also clog the pancreas. With insufficient enzymes to digest food, some people with this disorder may suffer from malnutrition.

Unfortunately, there is no cure for cystic fibrosis, although doctors can treat the individual's recurrent lung infections. In spite of the lack of a cure, progress has been made in extending the life span of children with this disorder. In the 1950s, most children with cystic fibrosis died before their fifth birthday. Now the majority live to about age twenty-one.

While cystic fibrosis is most common among Caucasians, sickle-cell anemia is usually found in people of African descent. One of every twelve African Americans carries the sickle cell gene, and 1 in every 650 actually inherits the disease.[8] To a lesser degree, sickle-cell anemia also affects Hispanics of Caribbean descent and some people of Arabian, Greek, Turkish, and southern Asian ancestry. Although it can be fatal, the effects of sickle-cell anemia vary from one person to another and from one occasion to the next in the same person. Many individuals with sickle-cell anemia live relatively normal lives.

People with sickle-cell anemia have an abnormal form of hemoglobin, the pigment in red blood cells. Ordinarily, these blood cells are round and flexible. In individuals with sickle-cell anemia, the red blood cells become sickled, or crescent-shaped. This sickle shape makes the blood cells more likely to be trapped in the spleen and destroyed, leaving the person with a shortage of red blood cells. Red blood cells carry oxygen to all parts of the body, and a decrease in their number causes an affected person to be tired, short of breath, and pale.

When sickled cells become stuck in blood vessels, they can block the blood flow to various organs, depriving these vital tissues of oxygen and resulting in a sickle-cell crisis. Such crises are often very painful and may injure the brain, lungs, and kidneys. If the damage is severe enough, it can even lead to death. As in the case of cystic fibrosis, there is no treatment that can cure the disease or prevent red blood cells from sickling. Doctors can only help to reduce the damage done by sickle-cell crises.

As illustrated by Tay-Sachs disease, cystic fibrosis, and sickle-cell anemia, many autosomal recessive disorders either are or can be fatal. In this respect, these diseases differ from autosomal dominant disorders, which usually are not lethal. With the exception of Huntington's disease, dominant genes that are fatal soon kill off everyone carrying them, leaving no one left to pass on the gene. But lethal genes that are recessive can be passed on from generation to generation through carriers, surfacing only when two carriers have a child with the disorder. Thus, fatal recessive genes are not eliminated from the population.

In most autosomal recessive diseases, carriers are not affected by the abnormal gene and are indistinguishable from individuals who have two normal genes. But in the case of sickle-cell anemia, carriers (under certain conditions) are actually healthier than normal individuals. Although having two sickle-cell genes results in anemia, having one sickle-cell gene offers a person some protection against malaria. Since normal individuals do not have the gene, they do not receive this protection. Although this protection may not be of much use in North America or northern Europe, it is very advantageous in tropical regions where malaria is common—the area of the world where the sickle-cell gene originated.

X-LINKED DISORDERS

In autosomal disorders, the gene causing the disease is located on an autosomal, or nonsex, chromosome. Thus, autosomal birth defects strike males and females equally. But when the problem gene is located on the X chromosome, the picture is very different. Except in rare cases, these abnormal genes cause defects only in males. Females may be carriers, but they almost never inherit the condition.

Perhaps the most famous X-linked disorder is hemophilia. In this disease, affected boys lack a crucial blood-clotting factor. Since their blood does not clot normally, even minor scrapes can lead to uncontrolled, sometimes fatal, bleeding.

Hemophilia caused great havoc among the royal

34

families of Europe during the 1800s and early 1900s. Because these families tended to intermarry, the number of female carriers among them was much higher than usual for an X-linked disorder. Since male heirs were needed for the throne, a fatal disease that struck only males had heavy political implications for entire countries, as well as for the individuals and the families involved.

The lives of Nicholas II and Alexandra, the last czar and czarina of Russia, were particularly influenced by this hereditary disorder. Their son was born a hemophiliac, and attempts to keep him alive consumed the couple, to the detriment of their ability to govern. Because he seemed to be able to stop the boy's bleeding where doctors had failed, the monk Rasputin gained considerable control over the royal family, a fact that greatly displeased the rest of the Russian aristocracy. Finally, undermined by their ineffectiveness and inability to govern and by political events beyond their control, the royal family was swept away by the Russian Revolution.

How is it that a hereditary disease such as hemophilia can affect males and not females? The answer lies in the fact that females have two X chromosomes, whereas males have one X and one Y chromosome. In all X-linked disorders, the gene that causes the defect is located on the X chromosome and is recessive. When a carrier female mates with a normal male, all of their daughters will inherit his normal X-linked gene. There is a 50 percent chance that these daughters will inherit an abnormal X-linked gene from their mother, but if that happens, the father's dominant normal gene will override the abnormal gene's effects. Thus, the daughters of a carrier mother and a normal father have a 50 percent chance of being normal and a 50 percent chance of being carriers, but none will have the disorder.

The situation is very different in the case of sons.

All sons of a carrier mother and normal father will inherit his normal Y chromosome. Sons, like daughters, have a 50 percent chance of inheriting an abnormal X-linked gene from their mother. But because sons do not have a second X-linked gene that can override the effect of the abnormal gene, any boys inheriting their mother's abnormal gene will develop the disorder. Sons of a carrier mother and a normal father therefore have a 50 percent chance of being normal and a 50 percent chance of having the disorder.

What if an affected male mates with a carrier female? This is the only way in which daughters can also have the condition. In this case, the father can only pass on his abnormal X-linked gene, so all daughters will inherit at least one abnormal gene. They have a 50 percent chance of inheriting a second abnormal gene from their mother. Thus, daughters of an affected father and a carrier mother have a 50 percent chance of being a carrier and a 50 percent chance of inheriting the disease. And the sons of an affected father and carrier mother have a 50 percent chance of having the disease and a 50 percent chance of being normal. For a number of reasons, however, it is unlikely that this will happen. Until recently, most males with fatal X-linked disorders didn't live long enough to become fathers. In the case of hemophilia, new treatments have changed this, and most affected individuals survive to adulthood. Even so, unless these men intermarry with relatives, it is unlikely, although not impossible, that the mother of their children will also carry the disease-causing gene.

Hemophilia is not the only serious X-linked disorder. Duchenne-type muscular dystrophy, another X-linked condition, can also be fatal. Boys with this defect appear healthy until they are between six and nine years old. Then, slowly, the child's muscles weaken, forcing him into a wheelchair by the time he is

Sex-Linked Disorders

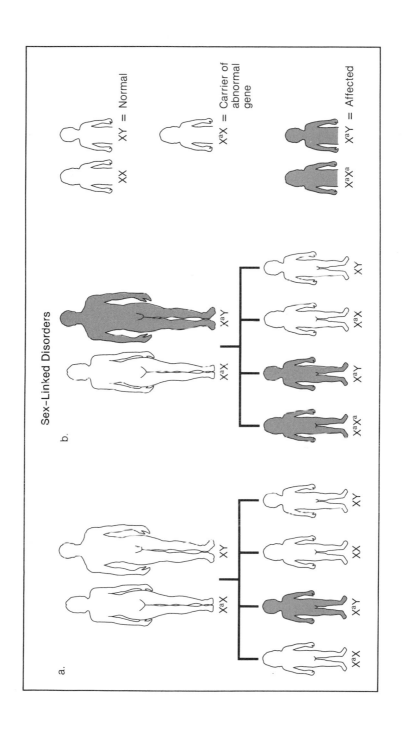

XX
XY = Normal

X^aX = Carrier of abnormal gene

X^aX^a
X^aY = Affected

a.

X^aX   XY

X^aX   X^aY   XX   XY

b.

X^aX   X^aY

X^aX^a   X^aY   X^aX   XY

a teenager. Unfortunately, this disease attacks all muscles of the body, including the boy's heart and the muscles used in breathing. These vital muscles often stop functioning entirely, resulting in death.

Not all X-linked disorders are fatal, or even serious. Color blindness, for example, has no effect on a person's health. Men with this disorder may need some help in choosing their clothes, but otherwise they lead completely normal lives.

2
ENVIRONMENTALLY CAUSED BIRTH DEFECTS

What exactly is the environment? In the case of an unborn child, the environment is the uterus and any substance that can enter the uterus. In addition to the nutrients necessary for the baby to grow, these substances can include such things as radiation, alcohol, drugs, viruses, and antibodies. When an infant is one of a pair of twins, the environment includes the presence of the sibling as well. Finally, the events a child experiences before and during birth are also considered part of its prenatal environment. Injuries suffered in the process of being born, for example, can cause permanent damage to the infant.

Some environmental substances, such as radiation and certain chemical pollutants, not only can penetrate the uterus and harm a baby's developing body but may also cause defects even before the child is conceived. Since exposure to radiation and some chemicals may result in mutations in a parent's egg or sperm cells, these substances can cause defective genes that are passed on to the next generation.

RADIATION AND CHEMICAL POLLUTANTS

In 1986, an accident occurred at a nuclear plant in Chernobyl, U.S.S.R., that sent shock waves through-

39

out the world. Although those most endangered were residents of the Ukraine, increased levels of radiation were detected as far away as Sweden and Norway. Could the radiation released at Chernobyl harm people as far away as Scandinavia? What would be the long-term effects of exposure on people living near the plant? At what level does radiation in the atmosphere begin to cause birth defects?

While not as serious as that of Chernobyl, accidents have happened at nuclear facilities in this country as well, most notably in 1979 at Three Mile Island in Pennsylvania. Residents of areas close to this facility feared they had been exposed to dangerous radiation. In Nevada, ranchers living downwind of nuclear test sites were exposed to higher than normal levels of radiation. Did this, as many claim, cause them to have a higher incidence of cancer and birth defects?

For a number of reasons, we may never get firm answers to these questions. For example, there are many problems in determining exactly who was exposed, to what degree, and what the effects of this exposure were. Prevailing wind currents can cause people living farther away from a site to receive greater exposure than those living closer, making it difficult to assess how much radiation a particular individual has received. The effects of exposure may not become evident until decades later, posing problems in tracing and documenting the damage caused. Also, accidents such as those mentioned have political implications. Governments, including our own, may be less than truthful in acknowledging the severity of the accident and may be motivated to minimize the harm caused.

There are some instances, however, in which the effects of radiation on unborn children have been clearly demonstrated. In 1945, atomic bombs were dropped on the Japanese cities of Hiroshima and Nagasaki. The damage inflicted on the unborn babies of pregnant women in those areas was directly related to how far the women were from the center of the blast. Pregnant women who were within one-half mile of the explosion and survived it had miscarriages; many of those who were 1¼ miles away gave birth to microcephalic children—that is, children with abnormally small heads and underdeveloped brains. Beyond two miles, the children were born healthy but had a higher-than-normal incidence of leukemia later in life.

Radiation has also caused birth defects when used to treat cancer in pregnant patients. In one study, over 20 percent of the infants born to women who had received cobalt treatment during pregnancy were microcephalic. Because of the high incidence of central nervous system defects that can result from radiation, physicians are now very careful about their use of X rays in pregnant women. (In fact, to ensure that a woman who might possibly be pregnant is not exposed to radiation, most physicians do not permit them to have abdominal X rays more than two weeks after their last period.)

Certain chemical pollutants are also suspected of causing birth defects. One of these chemicals is dioxin, a component of Agent Orange. During the early part of the Vietnam War, 11 million gallons of Agent Orange, a chemical defoliant, were sprayed over areas in which U.S. troops were deployed. Dioxin was an infinitesimally small part of this mixture, only about twenty-two gallons' worth. Dioxin is extremely toxic, however, and many Vietnam veterans felt that exposure to even tiny amounts of the substance caused them to develop cancer and their children to be born with birth defects.

Although this may be true, demonstrating it conclusively presents many of the same problems involved in documenting the effects of nuclear accidents. Not only is it a political issue, but other factors cloud the picture as well. For example, men who think they were exposed to dioxin may not have been, even if they were in areas that were sprayed with Agent Orange. Moreover, studies of the effects of dioxin often result in contradictory conclusions. Although the children of Vietnam veterans in Atlanta who claim to have been exposed to Agent Orange had a higher incidence of certain birth defects, no connection between dioxin and birth defects has been discovered in studies conducted in Arkansas, Michigan, Australia, and Hungary.

The effects of paternal exposure to dioxin on the children of Vietnam veterans may never be demonstrated, but other events have plainly illustrated the link that can exist between some chemical pollutants and birth defects. In the late 1950s and early 1960s, a manufacturing plant on the coast of Japan dumped mercury into the nearby ocean. The mercury made its way into the fish eaten by people in surrounding villages. The results were devastating—a heartbreaking syndrome of birth defects, including crippling malformations and severe mental retardation.

Although the dangers of exposure to radiation and chemical pollutants are frightening, these are not the environmental influences most likely to cause birth defects. Most proven cases of environmentally caused birth defects result either from maternal infections or from substances a pregnant woman has knowingly ingested. Sometimes the woman may have little choice in the matter, as in the case of medication that is vital to her health. Such drugs are taken with the knowledge that they may be harmful to an unborn child. In other cases, a woman may not know a particular drug causes birth defects or, if she is aware of the drug's dangers, she may not know she is pregnant. Finally, in the case of alcohol and illegal drug abuse, the woman

42

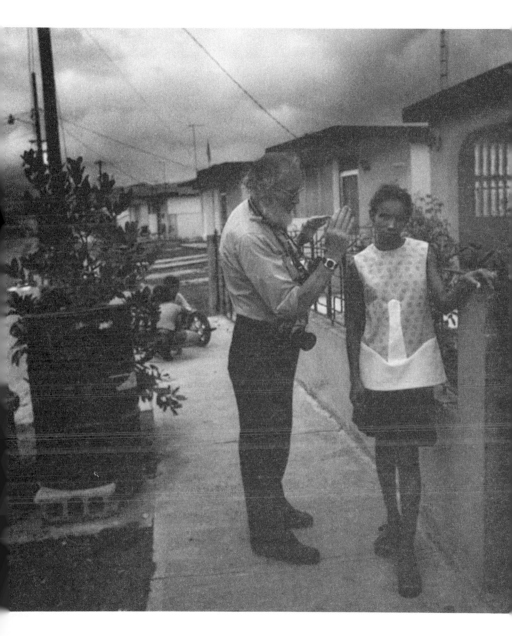

Mercury pollution was also a problem in Puerto
Rico. Here, a woman is tested for tunnel vision.

may be unwilling or unable to stop taking the substance, even if she knows it may be harmful to the child she is carrying, because she is addicted to the substance.

In spite of some of the problems involved in avoiding maternal infections and dangerous substances, the encouraging note is that, unlike radiation and large-scale chemical pollutants, we have some control over whether we allow them into the environment of an unborn child.

MATERNAL DISEASES

Certain infectious diseases can have devastating effects on the unborn baby of a pregnant woman who becomes infected. Rubella, also known as three-day measles or German measles, is one of these infections. Although rubella causes only mild, temporary discomfort to the mother, the disease can be very destructive to her baby's developing organs, resulting in blindness, deafness, microcephaly, mental retardation, cerebral palsy, and congenital heart defects.

The effects of rubella vary, depending upon when in pregnancy or in the immediate prepregnancy period the mother became infected. If rubella occurs within a month before conception, the baby has a 42 percent chance of being affected. This risk rises in the first trimester, the first twelve weeks of pregnancy. Fifty-two percent of infants born to mothers infected during that time have the full syndrome of defects. Later, as the baby's body becomes more fully developed, it is less vulnerable to the effects of the disease. By the third trimester, rubella infection in the mother usually leaves the infant unharmed.

Other infectious diseases, including toxoplasmosis, herpesvirus, syphilis, and cytomegalovirus, can cause defects similar to those resulting from rubella.

Cytomegalovirus, a flu-like infection, is particularly problematic because it is so widespread. Thirty to 60 percent of pregnant women have antibodies that show they have been recently exposed to this disease. Because it's so prevalent, scientists think cytomegalovirus may be a major cause of mental retardation, although this has yet to be proved.

Chicken pox, although not as dangerous to an unborn child as the diseases previously mentioned, can also cause defects. In this case, brain development is unaffected, but the baby may have facial or limb abnormalities.

In the 1970s, a new disease, carried by the deer tick, appeared on the East Coast of the United States. Called Lyme disease, it is now suspected of causing some cases of heart and brain damage in infants whose mothers became infected during pregnancy. Another disease, this one with a long history in the United States, has also just recently been recognized as being dangerous to unborn babies. Although erythema infectiosum, or fifth disease, as it is more commonly known, does not seem to cause birth defects, it can result in spontaneous abortion or stillbirth.

Finally, infections are not the only diseases that can result in problems. Chronic maternal illnesses, especially diabetes, can also cause defects. In addition to growth delays, the babies of diabetic mothers are more likely to have spina bifida, cardiovascular abnormalities, and malformed legs than are children of women who don't have diabetes. Fortunately, however, this risk can be reduced if the woman's diabetes is well controlled.

PRESCRIPTION DRUGS

As a market representative for a large West German company, Ulrich has to do more than just promote his product. He must first overcome the public's aversion to the way he looks. Although an attractive man in most respects, Ulrich lacks normal arms. In their place are two short, fingerless, flipper-like appendages, the result of a drug his mother took to control nausea during the early part of her pregnancy with him.

In the late 1950s, this drug, called thalidomide, was given to many pregnant women in Europe as a treatment for morning sickness. Initially, there seemed to be no problems associated with the medication, and it sold well. Soon, however, doctors began to notice an alarming increase in the number of children born with previously rare birth defects. These children either lacked arms and legs or had shortened and deformed limbs.

Studies revealed the cause to be thalidomide. Scientists also discovered that the drug's adverse effects were limited to the two-week period in which the baby's arm and leg buds normally form. If a woman happened to take the drug between days 23 and 30 of pregnancy, her baby's legs were affected. Between days 31 and 35, the drug affected the development of the infant's arms as well. By the thirty-sixth day of pregnancy, the baby's limb buds were formed, and their development could no longer be affected by thalidomide.

Ulrich's mother was not bothered by nausea until the fourth week of pregnancy. It took her a few days to get around to getting the medication. When she began taking thalidomide, it was the thirty-second day of her pregnancy, so her baby's leg buds had completed formation. His undeveloped arm buds, however, were still vulnerable.

Fortunately, few children were born in the United States with thalidomide-related defects. Because the U.S. federal government requires strict testing to determine the adverse effects of any new drug, tha-

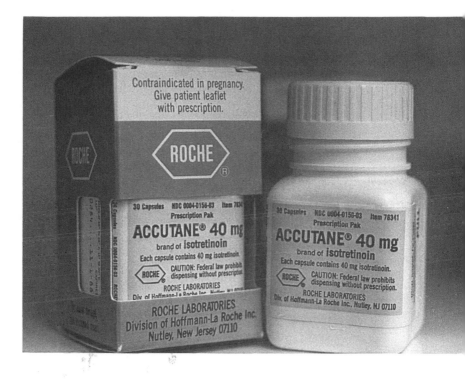

*Accutane is not vital to a woman's survival
and should be eliminated when she is pregnant.*

lidomide was never released in this country, although some pregnant women obtained the drug in Europe. Needless to say, as soon as its side effects were recognized, thalidomide was taken off the market in Europe as well.

Although thalidomide is probably the best-known teratogenic, or defect-causing, prescription drug, there are others that can also result in birth defects. One drug that has received considerable publicity because of the defects associated with it is Accutane®, a type of vitamin A. Used to treat severe acne, Accutane can cause head and facial deformities in an unborn child. A popular antibiotic, tetracycline, can lead to staining of a child's teeth if taken while his or her mother was pregnant.

More problematic are drugs that a mother must take for her own health but that may cause defects in the child she is carrying. Dilantin®, an anticonvulsant used to treat epilepsy, can result in malformed arms and legs and a strange facial appearance.

Anticancer drugs can be particularly dangerous to an unborn child. Many of these drugs work by destroying all rapidly dividing cells in the patient's body. Since cancerous cells divide at a faster rate than most normal cells, the drug targets them for elimination. However, normal cells of certain parts of the body, like hair and the lining of the mouth, also divide at a higher than average rate and are destroyed along with the tumor cells. That is why chemotherapy patients frequently lose their hair and have mouth sores. Unfortunately, because an unborn baby is growing so fast, among the most rapidly dividing cells in a pregnant woman are the cells of the baby she is carrying. The drug doesn't discriminate between different types of rapidly dividing cells, so the baby can be attacked as well, resulting in a high incidence of malformations and miscarriages. Methotrexate, for example, a commonly used cancer drug, can lead to deformities of the infant's eyes, ears, head, and skeleton.

UNNECESSARY TRAGEDIES:
FETAL ALCOHOL SYNDROME AND
DRUG-ADDICTED INFANTS

Mrs. Matthews had had trouble with periodic drinking bouts since she was a teenager, but it wasn't until she became pregnant with her third child, Darryl, that her drinking problem escalated out of control. Mr. Matthews, recently unemployed and despairing of being able to support his family, had responded to the news of his wife's pregnancy by leaving town. Frightened and furious at being abandoned, Mrs. Matthews disappeared too—into a bottle.

The effect of her drinking on the baby she was carrying was catastrophic. Like more than one third of the children born to alcoholic women, Darryl suffers from a collection of birth defects known as fetal alcohol syndrome, or FAS.

Infants with FAS are abnormally small at birth, particularly in terms of head size. Most have mild to moderate retardation and grow to be jittery, poorly coordinated children with short attention spans and behavioral problems. Some also have joint abnormalities and congenital heart defects. In addition to these problems, Darryl also has the narrow eyes and short, upturned nose characteristic of children with FAS.

The tragedy is that Darryl could have been spared all of this if his mother had refrained from drinking. Since the brain, heart, and blood vessels begin to develop within the third week of pregnancy, alcohol poses a danger to the unborn child almost from conception. Alcohol passes through the placenta unhindered. Therefore, any drink a pregnant woman takes is a drink her unborn child takes too. And since the baby is much smaller, the drink has a much stronger effect.

Although the babies of alcoholics suffer the greatest damage, even moderate drinking is suspected of causing learning disabilities and minor physical problems. The type and degree of defect appears to be related to the amount of alcohol ingested and whether or not drinking occurs in binges. Darryl's older sister, Lynette, has always been considered "slow" by her teachers. In retrospect, there is reason to believe that

Lynette may have been affected by the occasional drinking binges her mother went on when she was pregnant with Lynette.

Alcohol is the drug most commonly abused, but a pregnant woman's use of heroin, cocaine, or marijuana can also affect her baby. Infants born to heroin users are often themselves addicted. Although there is no evidence that heroin causes malformations, addicted babies may suffer withdrawal symptoms after birth that are severe enough to cause brain damage or even death.

Until recently, it was unclear whether or not a mother's cocaine or marijuana use affected her unborn child. Part of the difficulty in determining the effects of these substances was that past studies relied on self-reports to determine which women used these drugs during pregnancy. Obviously, since both drugs are illegal, many women may have been uncomfortable admitting they used them. In new studies employing urine tests to separate users from nonusers, it was found that both drugs influence an unborn baby's growth.

Women who used either marijuana or cocaine while pregnant gave birth to infants who were shorter and weighed less than the babies of mothers who didn't use the drugs. In addition, the children of mothers who used cocaine also had a smaller head circumference.

PROBLEMS DURING DELIVERY

Francine and Dolores are identical ten-year-old twins, a fact that surprises many people at first. Unlike most identical twins, it's easy to tell these two girls apart. Francine is an attractive, graceful child who loves talking to anyone who will listen. Her twin sister, however, presents an entirely different picture. Dolores can

50

This young boy underwent withdrawal at birth
because his mother was a heroin addict.

barely control her arms and legs and has trouble maintaining a sitting or standing posture. There is something wrong with her facial muscles as well, for she frequently drools and has trouble forming words correctly. Although Dolores is as bright as her twin, her difficulty in speaking and writing makes it hard for her to demonstrate her intelligence. Dolores has been this way all of her life. She was born with a form of cerebral palsy.

How is it that Dolores could be born with a birth defect while Francine was not? As identical twins, Francine and Dolores have exactly the same genetic makeup. Thus, any inherited genetic problems should affect them equally. Since they both developed at the same time and in the same prenatal environment, it's hard to imagine how Dolores could have been harmed by some environmental factor if Francine was not.

Although they shared the same womb, even identical twins do not develop in exactly the same environment, nor do they have exactly the same experiences. The human uterus is designed to hold one baby. With any more than that, conditions become crowded. Twins are placed differently in the womb; often one twin has more room than the other. And only one twin can be born first. In Dolores's case, these slight differences made all the difference in the world.

Francine, the larger of the twins, was born first and without complications. But then problems developed. Like 40 percent of twins born second, Dolores was in a breech position. Instead of headfirst, babies in this position are born backside, feet, or knees first. Because the head is the largest part of the baby's body, babies born with their heads last run the risk of getting stuck in the birth canal.

The girls' mother was already nearing exhaustion when it became apparent that delivery of the second baby was going to be more difficult. As labor stretched on, her obstetrician worried that the baby's brain might become damaged, either from physical pressure or from a lack of oxygen. Just as he decided it was time to deliver the infant by cesarean section, Dolores was born.

Unfortunately, the doctor's fears were justified. With prolonged labor, the oxygen supply to Dolores had become drastically diminished, causing damage to the nerves in her brain that regulate movement. Since Dolores was born with these structural defects, her cerebral palsy can be considered a birth defect. It is not, however, a hereditary (genetic) defect.

Cerebral palsy refers to the range of problems in movement and posture that can result from injury to a developing brain. Because our brains are not fully developed until approximately age sixteen, any damage to the brain before birth, during birth, during childhood, or in early adolescence can cause cerebral palsy. When injury occurs after birth, the resulting condition is not a birth defect. Unlike other disorders, such as Tay-Sachs disease, or phenylketonuria (PKU), which also involve damage to a developing brain, cerebral palsy is not progressive. In other words, the damage from it does not get worse over time.

3

DEFECTS RESULTING FROM BOTH HEREDITY AND ENVIRONMENT

Some of the most common birth defects result from an interaction between genes and the environment. As we shall see in the case of Rh disease and PKU, sometimes both the genes and the environmental factors are known. More often, however, exactly how these elements interact to cause a particular defect is not understood.

Lorraine's first pregnancy seemed effortless. Because she was only twenty-five and therefore not at high risk for producing a child with Down's syndrome, her doctor did not advise amniocentesis. Besides, there was no history of congenital defects in either Lorraine's or her husband's family. Thus, when their son Jeremy was born with a severe form of spina bifida, the couple was stunned.

Together, the neural tube defects—anencephaly and spina bifida—are among the most common birth defects in the United States, occurring at the rate of approximately one in every one thousand births.[1] Anencephaly, a condition in which all or most of the brain is missing, is always fatal. Spina bifida, a defect of the spinal column, or backbone, has varying effects.

Normally, an infant's spine closes early in pregnancy, enclosing the spinal cord. But for reasons that are unclear, sometimes this doesn't occur. In some cases, the resulting defect is so slight that it is not discovered until the child happens to be X-rayed for another reason. In other instances, a part of the spinal cord pokes through the spine, forming a cyst or a lump on the child's back. If deeper roots of the spinal cord are involved, the part of the body below the cyst may have no feeling.

In Jeremy's case, the lower part of his spinal cord was affected, leaving his legs paralyzed. He also has no bladder or bowel control. In one respect, however, Jeremy was lucky. Seventy to 90 percent of the children with severe spina bifida also have hydrocephalus, or "water on the brain." Fortunately, Jeremy was spared this complication.

Lorraine and her husband couldn't understand how such a devastating thing could have happened to their baby. Her doctor was unable to answer their questions with any certainty. In spite of the fact that approximately 1,500 infants are born with spina bifida in the United States each year,[2] researchers still do not know exactly what causes the condition. Since neural tube defects are rarer in some groups—blacks and Jewish people, for example—and more common among other ethnic groups, scientists suspect there is a genetic component to the disorder.

But there seem to be environmental factors involved as well. In countries where neural tube defects are more common, the incidence is three to four times greater among poor families than among affluent ones. And recent studies strongly point to a lack of folic acid in the mother's diet as a contributing factor.

In contrast to Lorraine, May wasn't surprised when her son Jimmy was born with a cleft lip and palate.

Since Jimmy's father had been born with a cleft lip, May knew there was a chance that her baby might be affected too.

"Cleft" refers to the split that occurs when the two sides of either the lip or the roof of the mouth (the palate) fuse incompletely. Some affected individuals, like Jimmy's father, have only a cleft lip; in others only the palate is affected. Like Jimmy, 40 percent of the people affected have both a cleft lip and cleft palate.

Since a split in the palate makes it difficult for a baby to suck, May has had to use a special nipple or syringe to feed her child. Jimmy's problems in swallowing also affect air pressure in his ears, making him vulnerable to recurrent ear infections that could lead to hearing loss. Finally, May has had to prepare herself for the fact that her son will have difficulty with speech when he gets older.

Although Jimmy may have inherited his condition from his father, there are also nongenetic factors that may be responsible. Five thousand children are born with cleft lip/palate in the United States each year.[3] In approximately 25 percent of these children, there is a family history of the defect. But in the other 75 percent, heredity doesn't seem to be involved. Some of the environmental factors thought to influence the development of cleft lip and palate include maternal diabetes, alcohol abuse, and treatment with certain anticancer drugs or seizure medications.

At almost three cases per thousand births, clubfoot is the second most common birth defect in this country.[4] Boys are twice as likely to be affected as girls, but no one knows why this is so. In the most severe cases of clubfoot, the entire foot is twisted inward and downward. If the foot is twisted far enough, the person must walk on the side or even the top of the foot instead of the sole. In less extreme cases, the foot may be sharply angled so that it points upward and

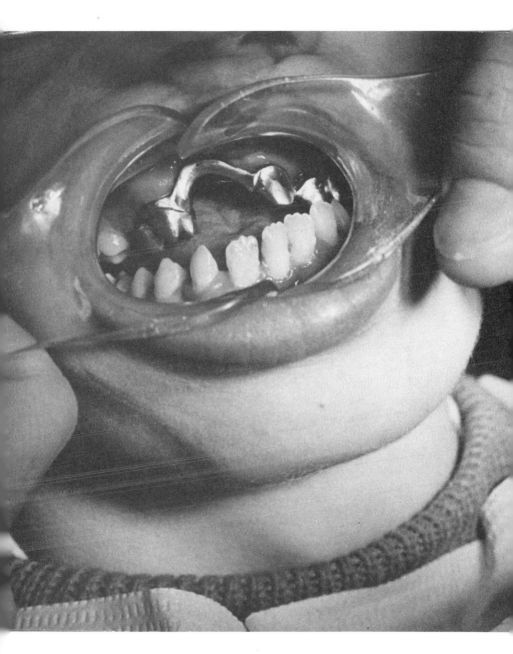

This cleft palate is being repaired.

outward, or the front part of the foot may be turned inward.

In the past, it was thought that clubfoot resulted from cramped conditions in the uterus. But now doctors feel the majority of cases are caused by a combination of heredity and unidentified factors in the environment.

Unlike spina bifida, cleft lip/palate, and clubfoot, in which the interactions of genes and environment are not clearly understood, there are birth defects in which the interaction is clear. As a result, physicians can now intervene to prevent these interactions and thus avoid permanent damage to the infant. One of these conditions is Rh disease.

The red blood cells of most people have what is known as the Rh factor. However, 15 percent of white people and 5 percent of black people are Rh-negative; that is, they do not have this blood factor.[5] People without the Rh factor are perfectly normal, but the absence of the factor can cause difficulties for the unborn child of an Rh-negative mother and an Rh-positive father.

Problems arise only when an Rh-negative mother is carrying a child who is Rh-positive, having inherited the Rh-factor from the father. The first time this happens, the baby is usually unaffected. During birth, however, some of the baby's Rh-positive blood cells enter the mother's bloodstream. Upon encountering the baby's Rh-positive cells, the mother's immune system recognizes them as a "foreign" substance and, in defense, forms antibodies to attack them. Once these antibodies are formed, they remain in the mother's bloodstream, poised to destroy any Rh-positive blood cells they find.

If the woman later conceives an Rh-negative baby, it will not be affected by these Rh-positive antibodies. Should the unborn child's blood have the Rh factor, however, the mother's antibodies will attempt to destroy this "foreign" intrusion. The effect of this antibody attack can be the destruction of the baby's blood cells, brain damage, or death before birth. Fortunately, doctors now have a vaccine that can prevent the antibodies from developing in the mother (see Chapter 7).

Neither Rh-negative nor Rh-positive babies have defective or abnormal genes. It's just that, under certain circumstances, the body of an Rh-negative mother can be a very dangerous environment for an Rh-positive baby.

This situation is reversed in an autosomal recessive disorder known as phenylketonuria, or PKU. In this case, there is no question that affected children have a birth defect, but before birth their mothers' bodies provide temporary protection from the damage that defect can cause (unless the mother herself has PKU).

Normally, the body produces an enzyme that breaks down phenylalanine, a type of protein present in many of the foods we eat. A single pair of genes is responsible for the body's ability to produce this enzyme. People who have either one or two normal genes can make the enzyme and have no problem eliminating phenylalanine from their systems. But individuals who inherit two abnormal genes lack the enzyme entirely.

Before birth, the absence of this enzyme presents no problem for an affected child. This is because the mother's digestive system processes food for both of them, and, in the vast majority of cases, her body is able to break down phenylalanine. After birth, when the child's own digestive system takes over, phenylalanine begins to accumulate in the baby's body.

This substance is highly toxic to developing brain cells and literally poisons the child's brain. Without treatment, infants with PKU begin to lose interest in their surroundings at about three to five months of age, and by the time they reach their first birthday, they are permanently retarded. Often, they are also irritable, restless, and destructive, and they may be subject to convulsions.

Brain cells are only vulnerable to the effects of phenylalanine while they are still developing. After that point, which occurs sometime in mid- to late childhood, the brain can tolerate high levels of this protein. The trick, then, is to protect the brain from phenylalanine until it is completely formed. This can be done by placing the child on a special diet (see Chapter 9).

Although there is no carrier test to determine which parents might be harboring the abnormal gene for PKU, there is a diagnostic test that can be given to an infant when it is two days old; it determines whether or not the baby is affected. Most states now require that all babies receive this test at birth.

Mike was born with PKU twenty-seven years ago. Although this condition can appear in any group, it is most common among blond, blue-eyed children like Mike. Placed on a restrictive diet until his early teens, Mike developed normally. Two years ago he married and now has a nine-month-old son who does not have PKU.

Shortly after Mike was born, his parents had another baby. This child, a girl, also had PKU. Like her brother, Monica was put on a special diet. Now a pretty and intelligent young woman, Monica recently married her college boyfriend. But at this point her path diverges from her brother's.

Monica and her husband are afraid to have children. Their concern is not that a child of theirs might inherit PKU. After all, both Monica and her brother have the disorder, and they've turned out fine. The problem is that, regardless of what their baby's genetic makeup might be, it will have to spend the entire pregnancy fed by Monica's digestive system—a system that is unable to break down phenylalanine. Even if the infant has the ability to produce the necessary enzyme itself after birth, its brain may be irreversibly damaged by then by the high levels of phenylalanine in the mother.

In the days before PKU could be treated, this circumstance was highly unlikely to occur. Since people with PKU were severely retarded, they were not sought as marriage partners and rarely, if ever, had children. Now there are women of normal intelligence who have PKU and want to have babies. If they are willing to go back on their restrictive diet, particularly if they do so before the child is conceived, these women may be able to bear normal children.

4

BORN TOO SMALL, TOO SOON

Low birth weight refers to an infant whose weight at birth is 2,500 grams (5 lbs. 8 oz.) or less. Although not a birth defect, low birth weight is a birth condition with ominous implications for the child. Two-thirds of all children who die in the first year of life are low-birth-weight babies.[1] Put another way, low-birth-weight babies are forty times more likely to die in the first weeks of life than are babies of normal weight.[2] Very low birth weight babies (3 lbs. 5 oz. or less) are almost two hundred times more likely to die.[3]

Some babies with low birth weight are underweight because they were born too soon—before the thirty-eighth week of pregnancy. Having had less time to grow and develop, they are smaller than full-term infants. The earlier the child is born, the less it is likely to weigh. Preterm (premature) births account for the majority of low-birth-weight babies.

Others may be full-term babies but small for their gestational (time-in-the-womb) age if growth was slowed for some reason during pregnancy. Babies can be both premature and small for gestational age; these infants are obviously at the highest risk.

Laura is typical of someone likely to deliver her baby prematurely. First of all, she is only fourteen. Al-

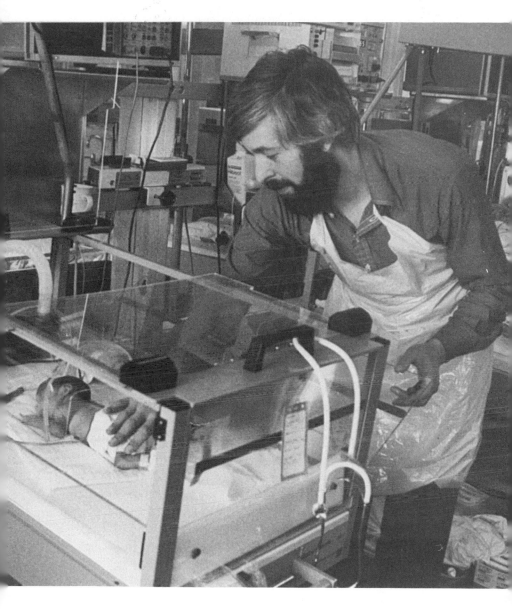

At this hospital in London, a father
helps care for his premature son, who
was delivered at twenty-seven weeks.

though women of any age can have a preterm baby, teenagers are especially at risk. Doctors think this is because an adolescent's immature uterus is more susceptible to early contractions. In any event, 20 percent of all adolescent pregnancies result in premature births, compared to 2 percent in the population as a whole.[4]

Other factors also may make it more likely that a woman will deliver too early. Women who have had many previous pregnancies, whose cervical muscles are weak, or who are carrying twins are also vulnerable. Chronic illnesses such as diabetes or infections in the third trimester can also predispose a woman to give birth prematurely.

In addition to the risk of preterm delivery, Laura is also in danger of having a baby who is small for gestational age. At fourteen, she pays little attention to nutrition and grabs most of her food at a fast-food place near school. Although she doesn't drink alcohol or take other drugs, Laura does smoke heavily. Poor nutrition, and smoking (as well as alcohol and drugs), can all influence birth weight.

Finally, even though Laura is six months pregnant, she has yet to see a doctor. Since she feels okay, Laura doesn't think it's necessary. Perhaps more to the point, Laura's family doesn't have the extra money for anything other than emergency medical care. There is a free prenatal clinic in her area, but news of its existence hasn't reached Laura. Unfortunately, although early and regular prenatal care can help prevent preterm births and low birth weight, many poor women like Laura have difficulty obtaining it.

Carol, on the other hand, sees her obstetrician regularly. Nevertheless, she too may be at risk to deliver her baby prematurely, although for very different reasons. Carol is a diabetic and has always had some difficulty controlling her disease. Her doctor suspects

*Nurses in this special-care unit
weigh a premature baby.*

that this may have contributed to the miscarriage Carol had three years ago, and he worries that the disease may affect this pregnancy as well, perhaps resulting in preterm delivery.

As in Laura's case, Carol may also be more likely than average to have a baby that is small for gestational age. Carol is forty-one years old. As a diabetic, she's very careful about what she eats. Nevertheless, her baby may not be receiving adequate nutrition because, in older women, the blood supply to the placenta may be less than normal.

Why does being born too soon or too small place a child at such risk? Preterm babies are not only tiny, but many of their vital organs are underdeveloped and unable to function properly outside the womb. Breathing, for example, can be a major struggle.

Twenty percent of all preterm babies have respiratory distress syndrome, a condition in which the lungs fail to expand as they should. Normally, the air pockets in the lungs are coated with a substance that keeps them from closing. But many premature babies do not produce enough of this substance. The result is that the air pockets collapse after each breath. Infants with respiratory distress syndrome usually need oxygen delivered through a respirator in order to breathe adequately.

Underdevelopment of the lungs is not the only problem that interferes with a premature child's ability to breathe. In all of us, respiration is controlled by the brainstem. In a preterm baby, the central nervous system is immature, and breathing is less automatic. The child may periodically "forget" to breathe, a condition called apnea.

Since an immature central nervous system also interferes with behaviors such as swallowing, a preterm infant may have trouble getting adequate nutrition. Many premature babies suffer as well from problems with liver functioning and/or low blood sugar. Usually, they do not have enough fat to maintain a normal temperature.

While in the womb, a baby's pulmonary artery and aorta are connected. After birth, the duct connecting the two should close. In about 20 percent of babies weighing less than 2,000 grams, this doesn't happen. Without treatment, this condition can lead to heart failure.

Many of these problems can affect the child's developing brain. Insufficient oxygen, low blood sugar, and the buildup of toxic substances inadequately handled by the liver can all result in brain damage. But the greatest threat to the infant's brain is that of hemorrhage. Nearly one half of all low-birth-weight babies suffer brain hemorrhages. Many of these episodes lead to brain damage and even death.

Babies who are full-term but small for gestational age have many of the same problems that preterm babies do, with one exception: they rarely have respiratory distress syndrome. Even with proper nutrition after birth, babies who are small for gestational age may not catch up with their peers in size and can remain short and underweight the rest of their lives. In contrast, preterm infants who survive usually catch up to full-term babies by the time they are two years old.

Compared to babies whose weight at birth is appropriate for their age, full-term infants who are small for their gestational age are more likely to develop learning disabilities and to have problems with attention span. Premature babies, especially those who are also small for their gestational age, are at increased risk for mental retardation and cerebral palsy.

PART TWO:
PREVENTING BIRTH
DEFECTS

The best solution to the problem of birth defects is to prevent their occurrence in the first place. Unfortunately, this is not possible in all cases, particularly not in cases caused by hereditary disorders. But many birth defects, including some of the most devastating, can be avoided. Defects that result from environmental factors, such as infections, drugs, and alcohol, can be prevented if women are aware of the dangers these substances pose and take steps to protect their unborn babies.

With the help of genetic counseling, couples worried about specific hereditary disorders can, in many cases, accurately assess their risk of having an affected child. Recent advances in prenatal diagnosis now make it possible to detect the presence of many birth defects before the child is born. In some cases, affected babies can be treated while still in the womb. In other instances, when the unborn child is diagnosed as having a severe and untreatable birth defect, the parents may use this information in deciding whether to terminate the pregnancy or in planning ahead for their child's special needs.

One of the most important steps a woman can take to prevent birth defects is to obtain good and consistent prenatal care. Doctors can prevent many of the conditions leading to low birth weight and congenital disorders, but not if the first time they see a patient is when she is ready to give birth.

5

GENETIC COUNSELING

Since we have no control over our genetic makeup or the genes we pass on to our children, we have fewer ways of preventing genetically caused birth defects than of avoiding defects caused by environmental factors. However, there is much that can be done to help parents concerned about genetic defects assess their risk of having an affected child. There are also several means available for testing an unborn child to determine if he or she has a birth defect.

Sandra didn't want to wait until she conceived a child to learn that it had Tay-Sachs disease. Having seen firsthand the suffering this condition causes, she decided not to marry Arnie if there were any chance she might have an affected child. When her family doctor told her that she and Arnie could be tested to determine whether or not their children might inherit the disease, Sandra immediately made an appointment for the test.

In spite of the fact that Sandra's younger brother had died of the disorder, neither she nor Arnie really understood what caused Tay-Sachs disease. The first thing the genetic counselor did was to explain to the couple that, because Tay-Sachs disease is an autosomal recessive disorder, a child can acquire the con-

71

dition only by inheriting an abnormal gene from *both* parents. Thus, both Sandra and Arnie would have to be carrying the gene in order for any of their children to inherit the disease. Since Arnie was also of Eastern European Jewish descent, there was a chance that he might be a carrier, even though the disease had never surfaced in his family.

Blood samples were drawn from the couple and analyzed for the presence of a particular enzyme. The amount of this enzyme that the body produces is determined by whether an individual has one or two normal genes. High blood levels of this enzyme indicate individuals with two normal genes; low levels indicate that the person is a carrier and has one normal and one abnormal gene.

In Sandra and Arnie's case, the tests results showed that they ran no risk of having an affected child. As their counselor explained, "Since only one of you is a carrier, none of your children can inherit Tay-Sachs disease. With each pregnancy, there will be a 50 percent chance that the child will inherit two normal genes and a 50 percent chance that he or she will inherit one normal gene and one abnormal gene. In the latter case, the child will be a carrier. But I want to stress," she added, "that since none of your children can inherit the two genes necessary to cause this disorder, none can be affected."

To the couple's surprise, however, it was not Sandra who carried the abnormal gene for Tay-Sachs disease. In spite of the fact that no one in his family had ever had the condition, the carrier was Arnie.

A carrier test is also available for sickle-cell anemia. In this test it is the shape of the red blood cells that indicates whether or not an individual is a carrier. Perhaps because sickle-cell anemia is a less serious condition, parents have been less motivated to seek this kind of information.

Carrier tests are only one aspect of genetic counseling. Different couples have different concerns, and counselors must use a range of techniques to help each arrive at a realistic picture of their situation. Some couples seek counseling because they have had a child with a particular abnormality, have family members who have a birth defect, or are from an ethnic group at risk for a particular disorder. Others are older couples, concerned because of the increased risk of certain chromosomal defects in mothers over thirty-five years of age.

The counselor's first step is to determine whether or not the birth defect in question is actually hereditary. Some environmentally produced defects closely resemble genetically caused disorders. On the other hand, the same genetic defect can assume different forms in different individuals. Similar defects can also be produced by different genetic disorders.

In some cases, the defect that has concerned a couple may turn out not to have been inherited, and the counselor can reassure them that they face little risk of having a child with the disorder. When the defect in question is hereditary, the counselor helps the couple assess the probability of having an affected child. Even in the case of genetic defects, the risk may be less than the couple had feared. In any event, they will have solid information to use in deciding whether or not they wish to take the chance.

As the advantages of genetic counseling have become more widely recognized, more and more medical centers and teaching hospitals have established genetic counseling units. Obstetricians and family doctors can help interested couples locate one of these units in their area.

6

PRENATAL DIAGNOSIS

As a result of their tests, Sandra and Arnie can go ahead with their wedding plans, no longer afraid that they will have children with Tay-Sachs disease. But what if the news had not been so encouraging? What if both Sandra and Arnie had been carriers? Is there anything they could have done to avoid having a child with this heartbreaking condition?

When it is determined that both individuals are carriers, the counselor explains to them that, with each pregnancy, they will have a 25 percent chance of having an affected child. But the couple can do more than just cross their fingers and hope. Procedures are available that can determine, after a child is conceived, whether or not that particular baby is affected.

The most commonly used test to diagnose an unborn baby is called amniocentesis. Through this test, more than 250 genetic disorders can be detected, including Down's syndrome, Tay-Sachs disease, spina bifida, sickle-cell anemia, cystic fibrosis, and PKU. Amniocentesis is performed in the second trimester, between fourteen and seventeen weeks of pregnancy, when about eight ounces of amniotic fluid surround the baby. A needle is inserted into the mother's abdomen, and one ounce of fluid is withdrawn.

Cells from the baby are present in the amniotic fluid, and these cells provide information about the baby's biochemical and genetic makeup.

To diagnose most conditions, the cells must be grown in the laboratory to accumulate a sufficient number for analysis. This means that the parents do not receive test results until seventeen to twenty-one weeks after conception. For parents anxious to know if their baby has a defect, this waiting period can seem excruciatingly long.

After much discussion, Janette and Bob (the couple discussed in Chapter 1) decided that Janette should undergo amniocentesis to determine whether or not the child she was carrying had Down's syndrome. Their hesitation was based on a dilemma many people face when considering diagnostic tests for their unborn child—what to do if the results indicate a serious defect.

The unfortunate truth is that, in the vast majority of cases, the only way to avoid genetic birth defects in a child already conceived is to prevent the birth of the affected baby by terminating the pregnancy. For some people, this alternative is morally unacceptable. For others, the degree to which the child is affected may be the deciding factor. Janette and Bob felt that in the case of severe birth defects abortion was justified. Their problem was in deciding just how severe was severe enough.

Unlike Tay-Sachs disease, which is not only fatal within a few years but involves great suffering on the part of the child, Down's syndrome is generally not a lethal condition. Moreover, the degree to which a child is affected varies greatly from individual to individual. Although children with this condition may be severely retarded in addition to having numerous physical problems, many people with Down's syndrome are only moderately retarded and can lead satisfying lives.

In talking with parents of some of the less affected children, Janette and Bob learned that children with Down's syndrome can be extremely affectionate; often they had brought real love and joy to their families.

After much soul-searching, Janette and Bob decided that they would take the chance and have their child even if it had Down's syndrome. But they also decided that Janette should undergo amniocentesis just the same. If the results indicated Down's syndrome, the couple felt they could use the time before the child's birth to prepare themselves and their families for the child's condition. If the results showed that the baby was normal, they could stop worrying.

Lorraine has also chosen to have amniocentesis, but with the definite decision to terminate her pregnancy if she is carrying another baby with spina bifida, or "open spine." Lorraine's first child, Jeremy, was born with a severe form of this condition. Because the bottom of his spine didn't close, the nerves governing the lower part of his body were unable to develop properly.

Not only do Lorraine and her husband, Ray, feel they couldn't stand the pain of having a second handicapped child, they also fear that the added strain would leave them unable to give Jeremy what he needs. Both Lorraine and Ray adore their son. In spite of his many physical problems, Jeremy is a bright, engaging child, and his parents want to give him the special help that he will need to reach his potential. But such help is expensive, in terms of time and effort as well as money, and Jeremy's parents have limited resources.

The risk of having a child with spina bifida is only about one in two thousand among people in the general population.[1] But the risk rises to one in forty among parents who have already had one child with the condition, so Lorraine and Ray have reason to be worried.[2]

In the case of spina bifida, levels in the amniotic fluid of a specific compound called alpha-fetoprotein (AFP) provide the clue as to whether or not the baby is affected. This compound is found in high concentrations in the spine. If the baby's spine has closed, AFP will not be present in the amniotic fluid. If the baby's spine is open, however, AFP leaks into the amniotic fluid, where it can be detected. Luckily, no AFP was found in Lorraine's amniotic fluid. Not only will she feel comfortable continuing her pregnancy but she will also be able to give Jeremy the brother or sister he so wants.

Janette was not so fortunate. Her test results showed that the baby she was carrying had three #21 chromosomes, a definite sign of Down's syndrome. Although the couple had already decided not to terminate the pregnancy whatever the test results, there were additional reasons now for Janette's unwillingness to have an abortion. By the time she received the test results, Janette was well into her second trimester. She had already felt the baby move and had begun to think of it as a separate person with its own identity. While abortion might have been an option earlier in her pregnancy, Janette could not consider it at this point.

In addition to diagnosing these defects, amniocentesis can also be used to determine whether or not an unborn child has been affected by its mother's rubella, or German measles. Rubella can result in a range of severe birth defects. Therefore, a woman who becomes infected with rubella during her pregnancy may want to terminate the pregnancy. But not all babies whose mothers get rubella during the first trimester of pregnancy (the most dangerous time) are affected. The amniotic fluid can be examined for the presence of immunoglobulin, a substance the baby makes to fight rubella. If this substance is not present, the baby has probably not been exposed to the disease, even if its mother had the virus while pregnant or shortly before becoming pregnant.

Recently, a new method has been developed for sampling fetal cells, which may replace amniocentesis. Called chorionic villus biopsy, it is performed during the first trimester, some eight to ten weeks after conception. At this point, the mother has just started to look pregnant and has not yet begun to feel the baby's movements. The procedure's main advantage is that parents receive test results at a much earlier point in the pregnancy. Not only is the anxiety-ridden waiting period reduced but, if necessary, the pregnancy can be terminated at a time when it is emotionally easier and medically safer.

In chorionic villus biopsy, an instrument is inserted through the vagina into the uterus, guided by ultrasound. Some of the chorionic tissue (a part of the placenta) is removed by suction. Since there are a relatively large number of the baby's cells in this tissue, additional cells do not need to be cultured, and test results are available in a much shorter time than with amniocentesis. Chromosomal abnormalities, enzyme activity, and sex can all be determined by chorionic villus biopsy.

But there are some disadvantages to this procedure. The risk of miscarriage as a result of chorionic villus biopsy is 10 in 1,000, compared to a risk of 2.5 in 1,000 with amniocentesis.[3] Nevertheless, for many parents, these risks are outweighed by the advantages of early results.

In addition to these techniques for sampling the baby's cells, obstetricians have two means of visually examining the unborn child. The most commonly used is sonography, or ultrasound. In this procedure, sound waves are used to outline the fetus. Doctors can determine a number of things from a sonogram, includ-

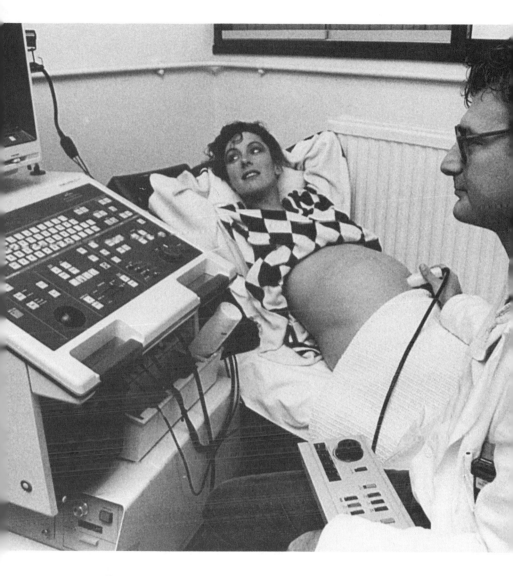

*Sonograms enable both the doctor and the
pregnant woman to see the unborn baby
(on the screen), and helps the doctor
determine if all is well in the womb.*

ing abnormalities in the size of the infant's head and whether or not the spine has closed. The size of the baby can also be compared with its gestational age to assess whether he or she is growing normally.

In another procedure—fetoscopy—a small tube is inserted through the mother's abdominal cavity. Using a specially designed light, the physician can look through the tube and see the baby. This procedure is particularly helpful in spotting congenital malformations.

Although very few birth defects diagnosed in an unborn child can be treated before birth, there are a few exceptions. Infants with two rare inborn metabolic disorders can be treated by administering vitamins to the mother during pregnancy. Another condition, hydrocephalus, has also been treated before birth. In this defect, commonly known as "water on the brain," the flow of fluid from the brain into the spine is blocked. As fluid builds up in the brain, it causes the head to enlarge. Physicians can surgically implant a shunt in the infant to drain this fluid and prevent further enlargement of the head. It is hoped that in the future, scientists will find ways to treat other birth defects during pregnancy, thus reducing the number of parents faced with the choice of abortion or the birth of an affected child.

Finally, it's important to realize that, as valuable as prenatal diagnosis is, it cannot guarantee parents that they will have a normal child. The tests available can detect a large number of birth defects, but there are many disorders for which there are no tests. For example, neither neurofibromatosis nor cystic fibrosis, two of the most common genetic diseases in the United States, can be diagnosed prenatally.

7

STEERING CLEAR
OF TROUBLE

Some of the most devastating birth defects result, either completely or in part, from exposure to particular agents in the environment. We can avoid many of these agents, thus preventing the birth defects they cause.

PREVENTING INFECTIOUS DISEASES

Even before she became pregnant, Darleen took an important step in protecting the child she hoped to have—she had a blood test to see if she'd had rubella, or German measles. Like several other viruses, rubella can pass through the placenta from a pregnant woman to the child she is carrying. Although the virus causes only mild symptoms in children and adults, it can have devastating effects on an unborn baby.

People who have had rubella cannot catch it again. Therefore, when the test showed that Darleen had had the virus in the past, she knew there was no danger that she could contract the disease again and expose an unborn child to the disease. For those who have never had rubella, there is a vaccine that can protect against infection. However, a woman should not be vaccinated during the few months before she conceives nor after she is pregnant. Since the vaccine is a weakened form of the rubella virus, an unborn child can contract the virus through the vaccine itself.

Developed in 1969, this vaccine has been an important step in preventing birth defects. In the rubella epidemic of 1964–65, twenty thousand children were born with defects caused by this disease.[1] Now, fewer than one hundred children are born in the United States each year with congenital rubella defects.[2]

Lyme disease can also cause problems in an unborn child. However, since Lyme disease is caused by a bacterium, not a virus (the cause of rubella, toxoplasmosis, etc.), it can be treated with antibiotics. Early medical treatment of pregnant women with Lyme disease is important in helping to prevent the development of birth defects in their unborn babies.

There are other infections that can endanger the child of a pregnant woman. Toxoplasmosis, syphilis, and cytomegalovirus can all cause problems similar to those resulting from rubella. Chicken pox, while not as dangerous a threat, may result in limb or facial deformities. With the exception of chickenpox and rubella, past infection does not make a person immune to the disease.

Genital herpes presents a special problem. Although an unborn child is not usually in danger of contracting the virus through the placenta, he or she may, if the mother has an active infection, become infected while passing through the birth canal. Herpes infections in newborns, whose immune systems are not completely developed, are often severe, causing brain damage and death. Fortunately, the spread of infection to the infant can be prevented with careful monitoring. If the mother has an active infection at the time of delivery, the baby is delivered by cesarean section, thus preventing the baby's passage through the birth canal.

In the past decade, a new infectious agent has developed that can infect unborn children: the AIDS virus. AIDS does not result in structural or biochemical abnormalities; therefore, it does not technically cause birth defects. However, since there is no cure for AIDS, babies born with the disease will die from it. AIDS-infected women who become pregnant run a high risk of passing the virus on to their unborn children. The only effective means of preventing this from happening is for women to protect themselves from contracting AIDS or, if already infected, to avoid becoming pregnant.

RH VACCINE

Rh vaccine can help keep the prenatal environment a safe place for the future Rh-positive babies of an Rh-negative mother. The vaccine destroys the Rh-positive blood cells that entered the mother's blood during the baby's delivery. With the Rh-positive cells removed, the mother's immune system has no need to develop antibodies against them. But to be effective, this vaccine must be given to Rh-negative mothers within seventy-two hours after the birth of any baby having Rh-positive blood.

AVOIDING TERATOGENIC PRESCRIPTION DRUGS

Although many people are aware of the effects alcohol and street drugs can have on an unborn baby, they may not realize that prescription drugs can also be harmful. When a prescription drug is not essential to the mother's health, it should be eliminated completely. One of these drugs is Accutane, or retinoic acid. Used to treat severe acne, it causes malformations of an infant's face and head. Pregnant women should avoid taking this medication, and women tak-

This boy was not born with AIDS, but
contracted it through blood transfusions
needed for treating his hemophilia.
Whether acquired before or after birth,
AIDS victims suffer the same,
as there is yet no cure for it.

ing retinoic acid should use effective birth control to ensure that they don't become pregnant.

Another prescription drug, the antibiotic tetracycline, can stain the teeth of an unborn child if taken during pregnancy. In most cases, other antibiotics that do not cause problems for the unborn child can be substituted.

When a specific prescription drug is necessary for the mother's health and substitutes are not available, a solution becomes more difficult. Diane's epilepsy is effectively controlled by an anticonvulsant drug called Dilantin. Some of the women who have taken this drug during pregnancy have given birth to infants with unusual-looking faces and malformed arms and legs. Now that she is pregnant, Diane is afraid to continue to take Dilantin. Unfortunately, other anticonvulsants may also cause birth defects. If Diane stops taking seizure medication completely, however, she may suffer convulsions, which could endanger both herself and her baby. As a compromise, her doctor has lowered the dosage of Dilantin during her first trimester, when her baby is most vulnerable.

When a woman is taking certain anticancer drugs that are known to cause or suspected of causing birth defects, the options are even fewer. Since the anticancer drug is vital to the woman's health and dosages cannot be reduced, the only way to prevent birth defects is for the woman to avoid becoming pregnant.

THE BIG NO-NO: ALCOHOL

Claire was in her last year of college when she became pregnant. Although she was aware of the devastating effects alcohol can have on an unborn child, she thought these problems occurred only when the mother was an alcoholic. Surely, she thought, the few beers she had at parties, after classes, or when she was studying couldn't hurt. She was surprised, therefore, when her doctor told her that the best thing she could do for her baby was to avoid alcohol entirely while pregnant.

Although it is true that the babies of alcoholics suffer the most extreme effects, even moderate or occasional drinking during pregnancy may cause malformations. Most physicians strongly recommend that pregnant women stop drinking entirely during the first trimester, and many suggest they refrain throughout the entire pregnancy.

Once she was informed of the dangers to her baby, Claire had no trouble cutting out alcohol. For other women, however, this is almost impossible. Alcoholism is an addiction, and many people can't stop drinking without help. Compounding the problem is the fact that alcoholics often have great difficulty acknowledging that they have a problem. If the unborn baby of an alcoholic woman is to be protected from birth defects, friends and family members of the pregnant woman may have to step in and see that she gets professional help for her addiction.

TOBACCO

Because smoking increases the risk of miscarriage, stillbirth, and low birth weight, pregnant women should make every effort to stop. Like other addictions, however, smoking can be a difficult behavior to eliminate. Even if a woman cannot stop smoking entirely, reducing the number of cigarettes may help to prevent problems for her baby.

CUTTING OUT
ILLEGAL DRUGS

The effects of heroin, cocaine/crack, and marijuana on an unborn child should be sufficient reasons to make

While waiting to see her doctor, this woman
reads about the effects of alcohol on an unborn
child. Even "social" drinking can be harmful.

all pregnant women stop using these drugs. For those who aren't addicted, these reasons may be enough. But people addicted to drugs usually find they can't stop just because there are good reasons that they should. Particularly at this time in their lives, pregnant women who are having problems with drugs should be helped to find treatment programs that will assist them.

Drugs that are taken intravenously pose additional problems for a pregnant woman and her baby. The use of contaminated needles is one of the major ways of contracting AIDS. Thus, pregnant women who inject drugs place their unborn babies in danger, both of becoming addicted to the drug and of acquiring a disease that will kill them. It is critical, therefore, that such women get treatment for their drug problem or, at the very least, that they avoid sharing needles with other drug users.

8

PRENATAL CARE

Preventing environmentally caused birth defects and low birth weight is not just a matter of avoiding substances that can harm an unborn baby. There are other steps a pregnant woman can take to protect her child. The most important of these is to see that she gets adequate prenatal care.

Many birth defects and other complications that result from a mother's medical condition can be prevented with medical care. Infections such as syphilis and gonorrhea can be treated; high blood pressure, toxemia, and diabetes can be controlled; and individuals at risk for miscarriage or other difficulties can be identified and monitored closely. But these things can be done only if the woman is seeing a doctor regularly.

Problems that arise during delivery that may require an immediate cesarean section are more effectively handled if the doctor is familiar with the woman and the course of her pregnancy. In other cases, premature births can often be prevented by medication if the start of labor is detected early enough. Obviously, a doctor is much more likely to spot preterm labor if he or she has had a chance to monitor the patient's pregnancy.

Tragically, many women with Rh-negative blood do not receive the vaccine that could protect their fu-

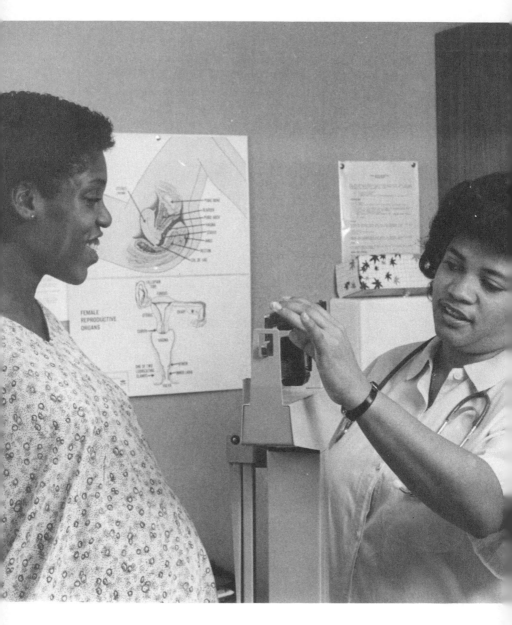

*Seeing a doctor regularly is one of the most
vital aspects of good prenatal care.*

ture babies from birth defects. To be effective, this vaccine must be given before the mother's immune system begins to produce antibodies, that is within three days of the birth of a baby having Rh-positive blood. However, many women do not know they are Rh-negative or are unaware that the vaccine exists. Others don't realize that the vaccine must also be given if the pregnancy ends in miscarriage or abortion, or they are overlooked by hospital staff for the necessary tests after delivery to determine whether the vaccine should be given. When a pregnant woman has established a relationship with her obstetrician, the probability that these things will happen is greatly reduced.

Finally, as Claire's experience illustrates, even women without health problems should seek prenatal care as early as possible. Had Claire not gone to the doctor when she did, she might not have learned until it was too late that moderate social drinking could harm her baby.

Many prenatal clinics go even further than providing information about substances that can endanger an unborn child. Often the staff can also assist pregnant women who are having difficulty eliminating alcohol, drugs, or tobacco to find programs that can treat their addiction.

PART THREE:
HELPING CHILDREN WITH BIRTH DEFECTS

While genetic counseling, prenatal diagnosis, avoidance of dangerous environmental substances, and prenatal care have all helped to reduce the number of infants born with birth defects, not all birth defects can be prevented. Even in industrialized countries with advanced medical services, three out of every one hundred babies are born with major defects. These children must receive the best treatment possible if they are to make the most of their lives.

With the exception of a few disorders, children with most birth defects can be treated or at least helped to cope more effectively with their disabilities. The outlook for each child differs, of course, depending on the severity of the disorder, whether it is the youngster's sole defect or only one of many, and what treatments are available. Some birth defects, such as cleft lip and congenital heart defects, can often be repaired. In the case of other disorders, such as PKU, damage resulting from the condition can be prevented. Even when the child's condition can't be corrected, however, it can usually be improved with therapy, enabling affected youngsters to reach their potential and to live lives that are as satisfying as possible.

Particularly important in helping newborn babies with serious medical problems is the Neonatal Intensive Care Unit, or NICU, a separate nursery at many hospitals for infants needing constant attention or special equipment to keep them alive. The NICU is staffed by a team of doctors, nurses, technicians, physical therapists, and social workers trained in dealing with the unique medical needs of preterm babies and infants with birth defects. The team not only cares for the baby but also helps the child's parents cope with the initial emotional trauma many experience, and it assists in connecting the family with community services that may be helpful when the child is ready to go home.

9

TREATING BIRTH DEFECTS

It is an accepted fact that having a birth defect will influence, to some degree, the course of an affected child's life. What is often not understood is how dramatic an effect it can have on the lives of those in the baby's family. The birth of an afflicted child is a crushing blow to the infant's parents. Not only must they grieve for the child, but they also must deal with often overwhelming feelings of depression, anger, guilt, and despair.

Depending on the severity of the birth defect, the infant's parents may find their day-to-day lives irrevocably altered. Caring for and treating a child with serious birth defects requires extra time and money, both of which may be in short supply. Sometimes, just taking the child to frequent clinical appointments, dealing with specialized medical needs, and seeing that the youngster gets to special treatment programs absorb so much of parents' time and energy that they have little left to give each other or the rest of their family.

If parents are too pressured by their own emotional, financial, and family needs, they will be unable to help their child get the treatment he or she should have. Thus, health care professionals realize that, to a large degree, treating a child with birth defects means treating the entire family as well. In the case of Jeremy, who was born with a severe form of spina bifida, his parents needed as much help as he did.

SPINA BIFIDA

Lorraine and Ray had expected the birth of their first child to be one of the happiest days of their lives. Instead, it was the most traumatic event either had ever experienced. From the moment their son was born, it was apparent to both Lorraine and Ray that something was wrong with the child. In the middle of Jeremy's lower back was a large oozing cyst, surrounded by sores. Although Jeremy's parents had no idea what the cyst was, they knew it shouldn't be there. One glance at the grim expression on the doctor's face confirmed the couple's fear that their baby had a serious problem.

Jeremy was born with severe spina bifida, or open spine. His exposed spine placed him in danger of developing meningitis, so treatment for his condition began almost immediately. Within forty-eight hours, surgeons had removed the large runny cyst and covered the wound with muscle and skin. But there was nothing they could do to repair the nerves governing Jeremy's lower body.

Over the next few weeks, Jeremy gained weight and continued to thrive. His parents' condition, on the other hand, went steadily downhill. The possibility that they might have a child with a birth defect had never occurred to either Ray or Lorraine. Now, stunned and disbelieving, they were having difficulty even grasping what had happened. Although the doctor carefully explained Jeremy's condition to them, they were too distraught to really absorb the information.

When the full implications of Jeremy's spina bifida began to sink in, however, the situation worsened. Assaulted by feelings of depression, guilt, and anger, Ray and Lorraine had little emotional energy left to console each other or to nurture their son. Ray, in particular, had difficulty accepting the fact that Jeremy's legs were permanently paralyzed. From an athletic family himself, Ray had secretly hoped the child would be a boy, and had looked forward to having a son who would share his interest in sports, a youngster who would be a football star, as he had been.

While Ray felt angry and cheated, his wife was overcome by guilt. Lorraine had carried Jeremy for nine months. If there was something wrong with him, she thought, it must be because there was something wrong with her. Either she had done something she shouldn't have when she was pregnant, or she hadn't done something she should have. Worse, she thought, maybe she didn't do anything wrong at all—maybe she was just defective as a woman.

Instead of being supportive, Lorraine's and Ray's families only complicated the situation. Lorraine's mother and father absolutely refused to believe that Jeremy's condition couldn't be cured. With enough money, they said, anything could be done. And they would be happy to provide the money. They kept urging the couple to see one specialist after another, doctors that weren't "incompetent quacks" like the "idiots" that had examined Jeremy previously.

Ray's parents denied the problem in another way—they ignored Ray and Lorraine. Even more upsetting, they acted as if Jeremy didn't even exist. When Ray's sister-in-law became pregnant, Ray's father said he hoped it would be a boy "so there would be someone to pass on the family name." It was painfully obvious to both Ray and Lorraine that Ray's father didn't think Jeremy was qualified to do that.

Although the hospital social worker tried to help Ray and Lorraine work through their feelings about

97

Jeremy's birth defect, the despair and anger the couple felt eventually proved to be too much of a strain for their marriage. By the time Jeremy was three months old, his parents had separated.

With her husband gone, Lorraine felt trapped into having to assume total responsibility for a handicapped child. She was frightened and furious, and the only thing that kept her from giving up completely was the support she got from the social worker at the hospital and the concern she had for her son.

In spite of the rough time Jeremy's parents had coping with his birth defect, they still loved each other—and him—very much. After a few months of living in a motel, Ray moved back into the house, and things began to look up for Jeremy and his family. Following the social worker's suggestion, Lorraine and Ray joined a support group for parents of children with birth defects. It made all the difference in the world! Hearing others express feelings that were similar to their own really helped, as did the concrete suggestions other parents familiar with problems of spina bifida had to offer. In addition, Ray and Lorraine decided to try marriage counseling as a way to put their relationship back on a sounder basis.

Through counseling and the support group, Ray and Lorraine began to perceive their son's problems, and their ability to handle these problems, differently. Once they began to see Jeremy as an individual with special strengths as well as special needs, they were able to focus on helping him make the most of his abilities.

Jeremy is now in second grade at a regular school, and his parents take pride in his good grades and his popularity. With his motorized wheelchair, Jeremy can go wherever he pleases. Two years ago, when he turned five, he began to take care of his own bladder and bowel needs. Since the nerves controlling these functions were affected by his spina bifida, Jeremy can neither tell when he has to go to the bathroom nor voluntarily control elimination. He's had to learn how to insert a catheter to remove urine, and, as he gets older, he will learn how to give himself enemas. To avoid accidents, Jeremy catheterizes himself according to a time schedule. Except for his wheelchair, he looks and acts like the other kids in his class. But most important, Jeremy is a happy, confident child who feels good about himself.

The initial surgery, the motorized wheelchair, and the self-catheterization techniques have all been critical parts of Jeremy's treatment. But Jeremy is who he is, as a person, largely because of the love and support his parents have given him. Had they not been accepting of him, it would have been very hard for Jeremy to have learned to accept himself. Thanks to the help his parents got, they were able to instill feelings of self-worth and optimism in their son. In a very real sense, then, a big part of Jeremy's treatment has been the treatment his parents received.

HYDROCEPHALUS

In addition to having a stable and supportive family, Jeremy was lucky in another respect. Unlike many children with severe spina bifida, he did not have hydrocephalus, or "water on the brain." In many cases, hydrocephalus occurs as a birth defect, but events after a child is born, such as meningitis or brain hemorrhage, can cause the condition as well. In hydrocephalus, the normal flow of fluid from the brain to the spinal cord is blocked. As fluid backs up, pressure inside the head is increased. If this fluid backup occurs before the cranial bones have fused, the infant's skull expands to accommodate the excess fluid, resulting in a permanently enlarged head. In an older child, however, the cranial bones are fixed in place and cannot move. As the intracranial pressure increases, the child eventually goes into a coma.

Doctors have developed a special surgical procedure to treat hydrocephalus. A plastic tube is placed underneath the skin on the back of the child's head. One end of this tube is inserted through the skull and into the brain. The other end runs down under the skin and into the child's abdominal cavity. This shunt, as the tube is called, bypasses the blockage and allows the excess fluid to drain into the child's abdomen. Doctors leave extra tubing in the youngster's abdominal cavity that uncoils as the child grows. Except for contact sports, children with shunts can participate in regular activities.

CONGENITAL HEART DEFECTS

Surgery is also an important means of treating congenital heart defects. Like hydrocephalus, there is no single cause of these defects. Often, heart abnormalities are only part of a larger disorder affecting the child, as in the case of Down's syndrome and rubella. Since there are many things that can go wrong in the development of the heart, the surgical procedure used depends on the particular problem. Surgeons may seal passageways that failed to close normally, repair holes so that blood can circulate properly, repair heart valves, or insert pacemakers.

CLEFT LIP AND PALATE

In recent years, plastic surgeons have developed new techniques that can improve and sometimes even correct disfiguring birth defects. Since facial abnormalities, in particular, affect the way a person is perceived

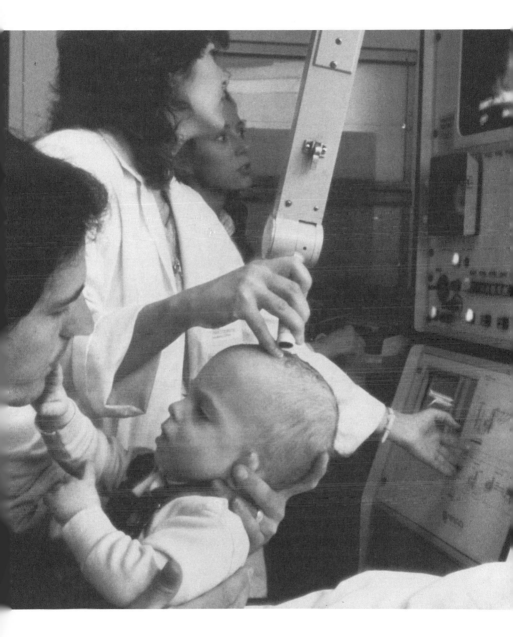

*An ultrasound is preformed on this baby boy,
who was treated in the womb for hydrocephalus.*

by others, surgical improvements can make a big difference in the child's social interactions and feelings of self-esteem. Jimmy's cleft lip and palate are definitely noticeable, and his mother, May, is very relieved that this defect can be surgically repaired.

Since Jimmy's father had a cleft lip, May has had some experience with her baby's birth defect. In Jimmy's father's case, however, the malformation was less pronounced. In fact, May was unaware that there was anything different about him until he shaved off his mustache. Then she could see the thin scar where the split in his lip had been sewn together.

Because Jimmy's cleft extends into his palate, the problem isn't as easily corrected. Joining his lip together is a simple operation, but closing the gap in his palate is more complicated. In a couple of weeks, when Jimmy is two months old, the doctor will do the first of two operations to correct this defect.

What concerns May is that Jimmy's cleft palate, even after it is surgically repaired, may result in other, more long-term problems. A malformed palate makes it harder to pronounce some sounds, and Jimmy's speech may be affected. At this point, it's unclear whether surgery alone will be sufficient to prevent difficulties in articulation. If not, Jimmy will need speech therapy. In addition, children with cleft palate frequently have missing, extra, or crooked teeth that may require orthodontia. May worries whether or not she will be able to afford this kind of expensive dental care if Jimmy needs it.

HEARING LOSS

Although Jimmy's hearing is fine now, his cleft palate makes it difficult for fluid in the middle ear to drain properly. This, in turn, leaves him more susceptible to chronic ear infections that can result in hearing loss.

Over one half of the children born with cleft palate eventually suffer some hearing impairment. Children with Down's syndrome have narrow ear canals and are also vulnerable to middle ear infections; more than 75 percent of these youngsters lose some of their ability to hear as a result. Technically, a hearing impairment that results from infections during childhood is not a birth defect. But certain birth defects make the child's hearing more vulnerable to damaging events later in life.

There are many instances of hearing loss that do occur as birth defects, though. Children whose mothers had rubella during pregnancy may be born deaf or severely hearing-impaired. In other cases, a hearing defect is genetically based. In fact, there are approximately seventy types of hereditary deafness. And children with malformations of the head and face may suffer hearing loss due to malformed ears. As might be expected, whatever the cause, a hearing loss that is present at birth or that occurs early in life can affect the child's ability to develop language.

The treatment of a child with hearing loss and associated speech difficulties depends on the answers to several questions. What is the cause of the hearing loss, and how severe is it? To what degree does this loss affect the child's use of language? (In some cases, children with more of a hearing loss may be less affected than children whose hearing is not as impaired.) Does the disability affect both ears, as is usual, or only one? Is the hearing impairment the child's sole problem or is it one of several disabilities?

In some instances, surgical procedures can improve a child's hearing, or at least keep it from deteriorating. Surgical correction of head and ear malformations, for example, may not only enhance a child's appearance but may enhance his or her hearing as well. Surgeons can also treat inadequate fluid drainage that results in dangerous chronic infections by implanting a tube through the eardrum. This permits the fluid to drain, thus helping to prevent hearing loss. Most of the time, however, the treatment of a child with a hearing loss consists of a combination of a hearing aid and speech therapy.

Hearing aids can raise the range of sounds a child can hear by 10 to 80 decibels. In many cases, the hearing part of the problem can be dealt with by providing a hearing aid and placing the youngster in the front of the classroom where it's possible to read the teacher's lips. But because of their disability, children with hearing impairments frequently have difficulty learning to pronounce words correctly. Often, they need speech therapy if they are going to be able to communicate effectively with others. This therapy is most helpful if it is started early in the child's life. Unfortunately, children with a greater than 90-decibel hearing loss may never be able to speak so that others can understand them. In this case, they are taught to communicate by whatever methods work best for them individually—usually a combination of sign language, lip reading, body language, and natural gestures.

CEREBRAL PALSY

Ten-year-old Dolores has problems with speech too, but in her case this is only one of the many disabilities she suffers from. Because of a decrease in the oxygen supply to her brain during her birth, Dolores was born with extrapyramidal cerebral palsy. As a result, she has extreme difficulty in controlling voluntary movement in much of her body. Her legs and arms sometimes jerk abruptly of their own accord, and she has great trouble maintaining her posture. With these problems, walking is almost impossible, and just sitting upright requires a major effort. Unfortunately, Dolores also finds it difficult to control her facial muscles.

As an infant, Dolores's cerebral palsy affected her ability to eat. The abnormal tone of her facial muscles and the problems of controlling her lips and tongue made her unable to suck or chew normally. Her parents needed training from a physical therapist in special ways to enhance her ability to perform these simple actions. At first, Dolores's mother had to hold the child's jaw stable and manually pinch her lips into a sucking position. As she got older, Dolores was able to learn to drink from a straw, but chewing remained a problem. Her mother used the technique of placing food between Dolores's back teeth; that helped because it forced Dolores to use her tongue and to move her jaw around to dislodge the food. Needless to say, the coordination involved in lifting a spoon to her mouth has also been hard for Dolores to master.

Dolores was able to get enough nutrition without needing a gastrostomy, however. This is a surgical procedure used for children who can't be fed adequately through the mouth. A small hole is made in the abdominal wall, and a tube is inserted into the stomach so that the child can be fed a liquid diet.

Like Jeremy, Dolores relies on a motorized wheelchair to get around. Her chair, however, is specially designed to help her sit upright as well. In addition to her wheelchair, Dolores wears braces, which provide stability and help control involuntary movements. Although drugs can sometimes be used to treat spasticity and rigidity, so far none have been found that are useful in dealing with the involuntary movements that afflict Dolores.

Dolores's twin, Francine, did not experience the difficulties during birth that Dolores did, and she has none of her sister's disabilities. Nevertheless, Francine's life also has been profoundly altered by cerebral palsy. Taking care of Dolores has absorbed the major part of her mother's time and energy, and throughout her life, Francine has had to take a back

105

seat to her sister's needs. Much of the twins' childhood has been spent taking Dolores to physical and speech therapy, to clinic appointments, and to be fitted for orthopedic equipment. Since there was no one to leave Francine with, she has gone along too. Often it seems to Francine that, instead of getting to play with her friends like a normal kid, she spends all of her free time in a clinic waiting room.

Not only does Francine resent Dolores for all of the attention and concern she receives, but she also feels her sister keeps her from having friends. Other children do not make fun of Dolores, but they find her drooling, unintelligible speech, and strange movements frightening and repulsive, and they often avoid coming to the house. When she looks at Dolores through their eyes, Francine doesn't blame them.

But Francine also sees a side of her sister that people outside the family don't. Sometimes, watching Dolores struggle again and again to do something that she herself could do without thinking, Francine's heart goes out to her. And, knowing the effort Dolores puts into everything she does, Francine cheers when her twin finally succeeds. She often wonders if Dolores ever wishes it had been Francine who got cerebral palsy instead, but if she does, Dolores never says so. When Francine looks at Dolores through her own eyes, she gets very angry at people who can't see how special she is.

Like many children whose siblings have birth defects, Francine has felt torn between love for her sister and wishing she could push Dolores's wheelchair in front of a car—and then feels guilty for having such bad thoughts and being such a terrible person. Luckily, two years ago, when Dolores got a computer, things began to improve. Unlike the majority of children with her type of cerebral palsy, Dolores is not retarded. Her speech problems, though, often made it seem to outsiders that she was stupid.

106

But with the computer, Dolores can communicate more easily, and Francine's friends are discovering that Dolores has a good sense of humor. With the ability to let others see her as she sees herself, Dolores has blossomed. When she becomes an adult, Dolores may be able to live independently in an apartment of her own by using the computer to do things like turn on appliances and lock the door. If you were to ask her, Dolores might even say her computer has been the part of her treatment that has provided the most help in dealing with her handicap

As extensive as Dolores's disabilities are, she could have had additional problems. Sixty percent of those who have cerebral palsy suffer from mental retardation, although the risk of this varies according to the type of cerebral palsy. One-third develop seizures at some point during their life, and 20 percent have hearing, speech, and language problems. Another 40 percent have some sort of visual deficit.[1]

VISUAL DISABILITIES

The most common cause of congenital visual impairment is not cerebral palsy, however; it is eye malfor mations and prenatal infections, such as rubella. Since congenital blindness can occur as an isolated handicap or, as in the case of rubella and cerebral palsy, in association with other disabilities, treatment depends on both the extent of the visual problem and the other handicapping conditions facing the child.

Even when blindness is the only problem, the inability to see results in developmental delays and difficulties in learning to speak. A blind infant is limited to touch and sound as ways of exploring the world. Thus, it's important for parents of a blind child to provide a variety of textured objects that can expand their baby's experience. Not surprisingly, blind infants are much slower than sighted children in beginning to move around their environment. Many blind children never crawl and usually don't begin to walk until they are two to two and a half years old. This delay in moving around also lessens their opportunity to explore and thus to understand their world. Parents can help to compensate for this in several ways. Talking to the child, even in infancy, and describing objects provides information about things beyond the child's physical reach. Equally important is to encourage the youngster to move about without being fearful.

Even in blind children of normal intelligence, self-stimulatory behaviors such as rocking, eye gouging, light gazing, and head banging can be a problem. Although their hearing may be adequate, blind children have difficulty learning to speak. The ability to pronounce words is based partly on being able to see how others move their mouths and then copying these movements—something a blind child can't do.

Treatment of a visually impaired child can begin as early as the child's condition is recognized. Even in infancy, there are things parents can do, as previously mentioned, that will help the child explore and get a better sense of the surrounding environment. Children can be started in a stimulation program when they are about six months old, and it's important that they are. By age two, visually impaired children are usually able to begin a special preschool program.

The degree of visual disability is an important factor in the child's further education. With appropriate visual aids and resources, children with a partial visual loss can often do well in a regular classroom. Children who are blind, however, need to be in a special class where they can learn braille, a system of raised dots that allows blind people to read with their fingers. Many blind children have also found computers to be a big help. Using a synthesized voice, some computers can even read textbooks out loud.

There are several aids available to help the blind travel outside the house. Many blind people use Seeing Eye dogs, while others prefer canes or sonar devices that detect objects. As is the case with those who are hearing-impaired, visually impaired children with normal intelligence and no other serious disabilities can go to college or learn a trade. Many grow to be productive, happy, and independent adults.

BLOOD DISORDERS

Blood transfusions can be vital in treating hemophilia and Rh disease, although the purpose of transfusion differs in each case. Hemophiliacs do not need whole blood; they need only the clotting factor they are missing. Injections of this factor can stop uncontrolled bleeding and have made it possible for many hemophiliacs not only to survive but to lead relatively normal lives.

In Rh disease, the mother's antibodies kill some of her unborn baby's red blood cells, leaving the infant severely anemic. In the past, many affected babies died before birth, and those who survived often suffered brain damage. With transfusions, however, the damaging effects of Rh disease can be prevented. In treating this disease, the purpose of the transfusion is to replace the infant's damaged blood with healthy blood. Because affected babies cannot wait until birth to be treated, transfusions are begun around the twenty-sixth week of pregnancy. A needle is inserted through the mother's abdomen into the uterus and into the baby's abdomen to deliver red blood cells, which help to lessen the baby's anemia. Several of these intrauterine transfusions are usually needed. After birth, the baby continues to receive transfusions for about an hour, until most of its blood has been replaced by healthy donor blood.

ENZYMATIC DISORDERS

With certain enzymatic disorders, the inability to break down toxic substances leads to a buildup of these substances, which damages the brain, causing severe retardation. In one of these disorders, phenylketonuria (PKU), this brain damage can be avoided if treatment is begun at birth. Children with PKU are unable to break down and eliminate excess amounts of a type of protein called phenylalanine. Physicians have discovered, however, that by removing most high-protein foods from the child's diet, the amount of accumulated phenylalanine can be kept to a bare minimum. It's important to begin treatment as soon as the child is born, however, since any damage that is done will be permanent.

During infancy, the child is fed a special formula that contains only small amounts of phenylalanine and normal amounts of the other types of protein needed for growth and development. As the child gets older, he or she can eat regular amounts of fruits, vegetables, and other low-protein foods but no cow's milk, meat, cheese, or poultry. When these youngsters are young and are exposed to only those foods their parents give them, they have little trouble with the diet.

As they get older, however, children with PKU become aware of other good-tasting foods that they can't have. No cow's milk, for example, means no ice cream, and no cheese means no pizza. Hamburgers and hot dogs are also off limits. Thus, many of the foods they see their friends enjoying are denied to children with PKU. Many children on this restricted diet find it very difficult to deal with, especially since it's hard for them to understand exactly how damaging eating these foods can be.

Doctors are not in agreement as to how long a child should remain on the special diet. Some think that at age six or seven it is safe to let the youngster eat normally, but others feel that the child should remain on the diet until age sixteen. Mike's parents wanted to be on the safe side, so they followed the doctor's recommendation to leave him on the diet at least until he finished junior high.

Mike had other ideas. By the time he was eleven, he hated the diet, not just because the foods were boring but because it made him seem different from his friends. Mike wanted very much to do what everyone else did after school—go to McDonald's and have a hamburger, a shake, and fries. Like many children on restricted diets, Mike started to cheat. When his parents discovered this, they tried to help him understand that it would be only a little longer, but a few years seemed like forever to Mike. It was a great relief to everyone when it was finally time for him to go off the diet.

MENTAL RETARDATION

Janette and Bob are well aware of the many problems their unborn baby may have to face, including an unusual appearance, heart defects, dental problems, possible hearing loss, and increased susceptibility to respiratory infections. What concerns them most, though, is the certainty that, as a child with Down's syndrome, their baby will be retarded. Because Janette had amniocentesis, the couple knows before their baby's birth that it will be a boy and that it will be handicapped. After much consideration, they decided to continue with the pregnancy and use the time to learn as much as they could about how to help their child.

Although mental retardation cannot be cured, Bob and Janette were encouraged to learn that there are many programs that can help retarded individuals reach their potential. What that potential is depends, of course, on the degree of retardation. The majority of retarded individuals are considered mildly retarded. This means that they can usually be educated up to about fourth-grade level. Most, about 80 percent, are able to find work, support themselves, and live on their own.[2] About the same proportion also marry, usually someone of normal intelligence.

About 10 percent of retarded people suffer from moderate retardation.[3] Although these individuals cannot live independently, they can be taught self-care and, if supervised, can also work at simple, repetitive jobs.

Unfortunately, the outlook for severely retarded individuals is much bleaker. Comprising about 5 percent of the retarded population, people with severe retardation have difficulty learning even basic self-care skills.[4] Often, they have other limiting conditions as well, such as cerebral palsy, hearing and/or visual handicaps, and seizures. Many severely retarded people are institutionalized.

Children with Down's syndrome may be mildly, moderately, or severely retarded, although most have moderate retardation. Most can learn to walk, talk, dress themselves, and be toilet-trained. Special programs are available, beginning at preschool, that teach self-care skills and help the youngster reach the educational level that he or she can achieve. There are also special work programs, sometimes called sheltered workshops, for adults.

Right now, Janette and Bob have their fingers crossed and are hoping for the best. Even though he will be born with Down's syndrome, their little boy will be lucky in one respect. He will have supportive, loving, and knowledgeable parents determined to help him make the most of his abilities.

Darryl has not had that kind of luck. His mother's

This young man with Down's syndrome pulls his weight around his house by helping with the cleaning.

drinking, which caused his mental retardation, has also made it impossible for her to help Darryl get the special assistance he needs. Early in his school career, a Head Start teacher noticed that Darryl was having problems. Because of his distinctive facial features, the difficulty he seemed to have learning things, and the little she knew about his family, the teacher suspected that Darryl might have fetal alcohol syndrome (FAS). She tried to have his disability diagnosed by professionals, a first step in treating any child with retardation, but Darryl's mother failed to take him to any of the appointments. When the teacher attempted to follow up, Mrs. Matthews got angry and became even less cooperative.

Darryl is in third grade now—for the second time. Because his teacher has trouble disciplining him, he spends much of the day in the principal's office. Darryl doesn't really know enough to go on to the fourth grade, but his teacher will probably pass him anyway because, by next year, he'll be ten and too old to fit in with others in a third-grade class.

It's hard to know to what degree Darryl's behavioral problems are due to his limited intelligence and the frustrations of being unable to handle his schoolwork and to what degree they are as a result of his chaotic and abusive home life. His older siblings have similar difficulties, and there is less evidence that they have FAS. Darryl is probably only mildly retarded. Even though his disability may be less, in some important ways, the circumstances of his retardation may limit him more than Down's syndrome limits Janette and Bob's son.

LOOKING TOWARD THE FUTURE

In the past few decades, great strides have been made in understanding, preventing, and treating birth defects. The more we have learned about environmental aspects that can injure an unborn baby, the better able we have become to avoid exposure to these substances and thus to prevent the handicaps they cause.

Unfortunately, preventing genetic birth defects has been more difficult. Genetic counseling can help a couple assess their risk of having a baby with an inherited defect. Once a child has been conceived, however, preventing its birth is the only means of precluding these defects in most affected children. This alternative is unacceptable to many people and a painful choice for those who do decide to terminate a pregnancy. It is hoped that in the future, fewer parents will be faced with such a difficult decision. Researchers believe that technology already in existence may someday be used to substitute normal for abnormal genes and thus correct some hereditary defects that are caused by a single pair of genes.

It is highly unlikely, however, that birth defects will ever be completely eliminated. Although many congenital abnormalities can be surgically repaired or limit the affected person only slightly, other disorders— such as those that affect Jeremy and Dolores aro far more serious and cannot be corrected. Special training, sophisticated mechanical devices, computers, and the support and encouragement of others can help children with severe birth defects live fuller, more productive lives.

Children with birth defects have much to offer. Perhaps the greatest challenge of the future is to provide them with the opportunity to make the most of their talents and abilities.

GLOSSARY

Amniocentesis. A prenatal diagnostic test in which a small amount of amniotic fluid (the fluid surrounding an unborn baby) is removed and examined for evidence of certain genetic birth defects.

Anencephaly. A birth defect in which the entire brain or all but the most primitive parts of the brain is missing.

Anticonvulsant. Something used to control or prevent convulsions (as in epilepsy).

Apnea. A condition in which a person periodically stops breathing.

Autosomal. Pertaining to any chromosome other than the two sex chromosomes (i.e., any chromosome other than the X or the Y chromosome).

Autosomal Dominant Disorder. A genetic birth defect caused by the action of an abnormal dominant gene located on one of the autosomal chromosomes. In autosomal dominant disorders, a person inheriting a dominant abnormal gene from either parent will have the disorder.

Autosomal Recessive Disorder. A genetic birth defect caused by the action of an abnormal recessive gene located on one of the autosomal chromosomes. In autosomal recessive disorders, a person must inherit a recessive gene from *both* parents in order to have the disorder.

Biochemical. Chemical interactions within the body.

Carrier. A person having only one of the two recessive genes needed to cause a particular genetic defect. Because carriers have one normal gene that overrides the effect of the abnormal gene, they do not inherit the birth defect. They can, however, pass the abnormal gene on to their children.

Catheter(ize). A tube inserted into the bladder to draw off urine.

Cesarean Section. An operation in which an infant is surgically removed from its mother's uterus; performed when problems with natural labor develop, posing a danger to the baby or the mother.

Chorionic Villus Biopsy. A prenatal diagnostic procedure in which a small amount of chorionic tissue (part of the placenta) is removed and examined for evidence of certain genetic disorders. This procedure can be done earlier in pregnancy than amniocentesis, but it carries a slightly greater risk of miscarriage.

Chromosome. Threadlike structures on which genes are located.

Cleft Lip/Palate. A congenital split in the lip and/or palate.

Clubfoot. A birth defect in which the ankle and/or foot are twisted abnormally.

Congenital. Present at or before birth.

Decibel. A unit for measuring the loudness of sound.

Dominant Gene. A gene whose action can override that of another gene.

117

Dwarfism. Abnormally short stature.

Enzyme. A protein produced by the body that increases the rate of certain chemical reactions in the cell.

FAS. Fetal alcohol syndrome, a collection of physical and mental defects caused by prenatal exposure to alcohol.

Fetoscopy. The insertion of a tube containing a light into the womb to allow the physician to visually examine an unborn baby.

Gene. The unit of DNA that carries instructions for the manufacture of a specific protein needed to build or run the body.

Genetic. Caused by or arising from the action of genes.

Hydrocephalus(ic). Commonly known as "water on the brain"; a condition in which the flow of fluid in the brain becomes obstructed, causing the head to become enlarged.

Meningitis. An inflammation of the protective layers surrounding the spinal cord.

Mental Retardation. Abnormally low intelligence. To be considered mentally retarded, a person must function intellectually at a level that is more than two standard deviations below the norm, must have evidenced retardation before age eighteen, and must be impaired in his or her ability to adapt to the environment.

Microcephaly(ic). An abnormally small head.

Miscarriage. The body's ending of a pregnancy before the fetus can survive on its own, resulting in the death of the fetus.

Mucus. Secretions produced by membranes in the

body. Their function is to moisten and protect the membranes.

Mutation. A change or alteration in the structure of a gene.

Nondisjunction. The failure of a pair of chromosomes to separate during cell division, resulting in an unequal number of chromosomes in the newly formed cells.

Orthodontia. The correction of teeth placement by means of braces, etc.

Orthopedics. Correcting or preventing bone or skeletal deformities.

Prenatal. Before birth.

Progressive. Continuing or getting worse over time.

Recessive Gene. A gene whose action can be over-ridden by that of another gene.

Sonography. The use of ultrasound to provide an outline of an unborn baby. The procedure allows a physician to visualize the development of the infant's spine, to measure head size, and to determine the child's sex.

Sway-backed. A curvature of the back that makes the buttocks protrude.

Teratogenic. Any substance in the environment capable of causing birth defects.

Ultrasound. High-frequency sound waves above the range humans can hear.

X-linked (or Sex-linked) Disorder. A genetic birth defect caused by the action of an abnormal recessive gene located on the X chromosome. Usually, only males inherit the condition, although females may be carriers.

SOURCE NOTES

Introduction:

1. March of Dimes Foundation, *Genetic Counseling.*
2. March of Dimes, Public Information Sheet.

Chapter 1:

1. E. J. Savitz and E. A. Wyatt, "Fulfilling Their Promise," *Barron's*, 25 September 1989, pp. 6–26.
2. M. L. Batshaw and Y. M. Perret, *Children with Handicaps: A Medical Primer,* 2nd ed. (Baltimore: Paul H. Brookes Publishing Company, 1986), p. 7.
3. Ibid.
4. Ibid., p. 8.
5. J. Adler, "Cause for Concern—and Optimism," *Newsweek*, 16 March 1987, pp. 63–66.
6. March of Dimes, Public Health Education Information Sheet.
7. G. Kolata, "A New Approach to Cystic Fibrosis," *Science* 228 (1985) pp. 168–168.
8. March of Dimes, Public Health Education Information Sheet.

Chapter 3:

1. J. Adler, "Cause for Concern—and Optimism," *Newsweek,* 16 March 1987, pp. 63–66.
2. March of Dimes, Public Health Information Sheet.

3. March of Dimes, Public Health Information Sheet.
4. J. Adler, "Cause for Concern—and Optimism".
5. March of Dimes, Public Health Information Sheet.

Chapter 4:

1. The Greater New York March of Dimes, *The Campaign for Healthier Babies: Fighting the Problem of Low Birthweight in New York City.*
2. Ibid.
3. Ibid.
4. M. L. Batshaw and Y. M. Perret, *Children with Handicaps: A Medical Primer,* 2nd ed. (Baltimore: Paul H. Brookes Publishing Company, 1986), p. 86.

Chapter 6:

1. March of Dimes, Public Health Education Sheet.
2. Ibid.
3. M. L. Batshaw and Y. M. Perret, *Children with Handicaps: A Medical Primer,* 2nd ed. (Baltimore: Paul H. Brookes Publishing Company, 1986), p. 30.

Chapter 7:

1. March of Dimes, Public Health Education Sheet.
2. M. L. Batshaw and Y. M. Perret, *Children with Handicaps: A Medical Primer,* 2nd ed. (Baltimore: Paul H. Brookes Publishing Company, 1986), p. 49.

Chapter 9:

1. M. L. Batshaw and Y. M. Perret, *Children with Handicaps: A Medical Primer,* 2nd ed. Baltimore: Paul H. Brookes Publishing Company, 1986), pp. 308–310.
2. Ibid., p. 195.
3. Ibid.
4. Ibid., p. 196.

FOR FURTHER READING

Apgar, Virginia. *Is My Baby All Right?: A Guide to Birth Defects.* New York: Trident Press, 1972.

Howell, Michael, and Peter Ford. *The True History of the Elephant Man.* London: Allison and Busby, Ltd., 1980.

Norwood, Christopher. *At Highest Risk: Environmental Hazards to Young and Unborn Children.* New York: McGraw-Hill Book Company, 1980.

INDEX

Page numbers in *italics* refer to illustrations.

Speech difficulties, 56,
102, 103, 104, 107,
108
Sperm, 15, 17, 28, 39
Spina bifida, 45, 54–55,
74, 76–77
treatment of, 96–
99
Spontaneous abortion,
45
Stillbirths, 45, 86
Syphilis, 44, 82, 89

Tay-Sachs disease, 22,
28–31, 33, 53, 71–72,
74, 75
Tetracycline, 48, 85
Thalidomide, 46–47
Three Mile Island, 40
Toxemia, 89
Toxoplasmosis, 44, 82

Turner's syndrome, 20–
21
Twins, 39, 50–53, 64

Ultrasound, 78–80, *79,
101*

Visual impairment, 9, 38,
44, 107–9

"Water on brain," 9, 55,
80, 99–100, *101*

X chromosomes, 14–15,
16, 20–22, 23
disorders linked to,
34–38
X rays, 41

Y chromosomes, 14–15,
16, 21–22, 35, 36

ABOUT THE AUTHOR

KAREN GRAVELLE, PhD, MSW, formerly worked as a psychotherapist with handicapped children. She is now a free-lance writer specializing in books for adolescents and lives in New York City.

WITHDRAWN